"One of the many things I have always loved about Rick Bezet is the fact that he dreams big dreams. In fact, sometimes he dreams impossible dreams, but he remains undaunted by that and stays the course. One of those big dreams is to reach every person in the state of Arkansas with the Good News that God loves them and is for them. Another of his big dreams is to remind you that you were also made for a purpose, and the God who made you wants to dream big dreams with you! I highly recommend *Be Real* to you and to anyone feeling lonely or overwhelmed, caught in a trap, or sidelined by life's unfortunate events."

—**John Maxwell,** *New York Times* bestselling auth EQUIP

"There are few things in life more freeing th icity and sincerity—and I can't think of a ow you how. With candor, clarity, biblic his book will put life back into your soul a closer walk with God."

—**Chris Hodges,** pastor of Churc ands; author of *Fresh Air*

"Our generation is blessed to have a great man of God like Rick Bezet. His humility and vulnerability make him an easy leader to look up to. And through his experiences we can learn how to *Be Real* and discover the grace of God that can only come through an honest and transparent life."

—**Steven Furtick,** lead pastor of Elevation Church; *New York Times* bestselling author

"As humans, we can waste a lot of time and energy pursuing our own plans in life, only to wind up frustrated and disappointed. With humor and transparency, Pastor Rick challenges you to throw off every hindrance and embrace change so you may step into all that God has purposed for you."

—**Christine Caine,** founder of The A21 Campaign; bestselling author of *Undaunted*

"Why do people wear masks? Why is authenticity such a challenge for Christians? These are important concepts that my friend Rick Bezet addresses in *Be Real*. I'm convinced that if pulpits and pews were filled with honest people, the church would be healthier. We must learn to be real—with God, ourselves, and others. Only then will we walk in true freedom."

—**James Robison,** founder and president of LIFE Outreach International

"Pastor Rick Bezet delivers a bold and thought-provoking message to be real and to overcome the fears and social pressures that prevent us from achieving greatness. In his new book *Be Real: Because Fake Is Exhausting*, Pastor Rick encourages the reader to stand proud and unashamed of their imperfections so that they can walk into the destiny for which God has called them. There is so much pressure on the body of Christ to appear perfect and without fault, but the only true strength comes from acknowledging one's weaknesses and calling upon the Lord for guidance and grace. We as believers should welcome an open and honest dialogue of the daily challenges that try to bring us down, so that we may lift each other up and grow as a whole. I recommend this book to believers new and old who are looking to shed their masks and live a life of unshakable confidence and unending potential."

—**Matthew Barnett,** cofounder of the Los Angeles Dream Center

"People like Rick Bezet who find a need and fill it and who find a hurt and heal it are always going to be special to me. While working tirelessly to turn his world around for the kingdom of God, Rick has remained humble, not taking himself too seriously, yet taking God's vision for him to reach the unchurched, the forgotten, and the hurting very seriously. I recommend *Be Real* to anybody who is unsatisfied with where life is going and is ready for a change. I recommend *Be Real* if you are tired of living your life without purpose or direction or if you feel stuck in a dead-end job or trapped in superficial relationships. And I recommend *Be Real* if you've fallen into the danger zone of focusing on your own needs or on finding someone to love you, when the best thing you could do for yourself is to notice other people, love others, and take the attention off yourself for a while. *Be Real* hits hard, and it hits home. But true to form for Rick Bezet, he shows a way out, and it's do-able—but you have to be willing to take the first step."

—**Tommy Barnett,** senior pastor of Phoenix First Assembly; founder of the Los Angeles Dream Center

"How much time do you spend trying to manage how others perceive you? Most of us like to think that we're able to keep up appearances, but the truth is that we probably aren't fooling anybody. Even if we do fool some people, we can't keep it up forever. Have you ever wished that you could just be you? My friend Rick has written this book as a powerful reminder that knowing God means having the freedom to be real. Check out *Be Real*, and stop faking it for good."

—**Greg Surratt,** senior pastor of Seacoast Church; author of *Ir-Rev-Rend*

"*Be Real* is an honest, challenging, and inspiring look at what it means to live an authentic life. In a world that measures value and success largely by performance and appearance, Rick shares a refreshing reminder of God's unconditional love and grace in a lighthearted and life-giving way. *Be Real* dares readers to stop hiding behind the facades and fears that hold them back and to start walking in the freedom God intends for us."

—**John Siebeling,** lead pastor of The Life Church of Memphis; author of *Momentum*

"Rick has an easy-to-read style that is humor-infused yet straight to the point! Like watching a compelling movie from your easy chair, Rick's stories and words will pull you in, in a comfortable and easy-to-absorb way. This is a book you'll want to buy three copies of and give to your closest friends!"

—**Matt Keller,** lead pastor of Next Level Church, Ft. Myers, FL; author of *God of the Underdogs*

"Rick Bezet has pulled back a curtain on the secret and highly destructive ways of too many professing Christian families. Is it any wonder that the majority of young people leave the church when they leave home? *Be Real* is not so much an exposé as it is a helpful guide on how we can be ourselves without succumbing to the pressures of false fronts and illusory images. As a minister to young people for much of my forty-year career, I can tell you that phoniness in the church is the number one reason congregations fail. *Be Real* is exactly the kind of message we need to become the people we were meant to be—ourselves!"

—**Willie George,** senior pastor of Church on the Move

"'Real' is what describes Rick Bezet. I have known him, observed him, pastored him, and now admired him for almost thirty years. He and Michelle simply live the life they expound. Their children are blessed, their marriage is blessed, and the great New Life Church is blessed by their example. I don't know what other people call 'real,' but that what I call it! Out of that 'real' comes 'rest.' Rick knows who he is and communicates that with authenticity every time he ministers. Grab on to 'real' and hang on—it may shake you, but it *will* shape you. *You* can start being real today, and your life and ministry will be totally redirected!"

—**Larry Stockstill,** pastor emeritus of Bethany World Prayer Center; director of the Surge Project

"*Be Real* is an inspiring book! I can't think of many things worse than going through life faking it. Faking it is so draining. Pastor Rick's book refreshes and encourages! In a world that says fake it, fake it, fake it, Pastor Rick counters popular culture and shares life-changing insight on why we must *Be Real*."

—**Herbert Cooper,** lead pastor of People's Church

"Rick Bezet has been 'real' as long as I have known him. This collection of his experiences and insights will challenge you to be real with yourself and real with God. You will not be able to put it down or read it only once. As you read, you will think of people in your life who fit Rick's experiences and want to buy them a copy. Get ready for God to show you the side of himself that loves you unconditionally, his one-of-a-kind purpose for you, and a great example of what it's like to live for him."

—**Joe Champion,** senior pastor of Celebration Church

"Rick Bezet is one of those guys you always want to hang out with. He is funny, easygoing, and genuine. He is true to who God has called him to be. *Be Real* will inspire you to live the same. This book will free you up!"

—**Stovall Weems,** lead pastor of Celebration Church

"When we were first introduced to *Be Real: Because Fake Is Exhausting*, we were intrigued by the concept. Our interest quickly turned to excitement as we explored the content on these pages. We can assure you that this book is not full of worn-out clichés about being 'real.' Sharing from Scripture and personal experience—examining what he did wrong as often as what he did right—Rick presents a compelling and empowering case for authenticity. Get this book today."

—**John and Lisa Bevere,** authors and ministers, Messenger International

"If we are going to fulfill our God-given potential, we will have to be the 'real' us. If we are going to have friendships that last, we have to be 'real.' In an era where authenticity is rare and pretense is the norm, Rick Bezet has written a book that will give all of us hope as well as practical steps for living an authentic life. You will laugh and be encouraged as you read through the pages of this great book! It will take courage to be the real you, and this book will help you as you walk it out. This is a great book for small groups to use to encourage genuine community!"

—**Holly Wagner,** author of *GodChicks*;
founder of GodChicks women's ministry

"There is nothing exhausting about reading this book. Rick has the unique ability to share the truth in a way that challenges you and makes you laugh at the same time. This book will help every reader recognize that it's okay to be real with others and that when we choose to be real, life becomes more enjoyable and relationships become more meaningful. Buy a copy for yourself and then one for every friend you have!"

—**Randy Bezet,** lead pastor of Bayside Community Church

"In a culture where the perceptions formed by first impressions are everything and posture and pretension are paramount, *Be Real* is the real thing the church needs right now."

—**Mike Kai,** senior pastor of Inspire Church

"Rick's book *Be Real* has given us the shortcut to an uncomplicated life. *Be Real* has taken the pressure off so you can just be yourself. You are the best you God has ever created. This book was written by 'the real deal,' Rick Bezet. Thanks for the simple truth that can transform your life."

—**Pastor Scott Hornsby,** senior pastor of Fellowship Church Zachary

"Every time I'm around Rick Bezet, I get inspired. He is the kind of encourager who makes me feel like I'm the best pastor in the world. In his book *Be Real*, Rick inspires each of us to take action. Whether you need to grow in your faith, begin to dream again, or learn the irreplaceable quality of encouraging others, this book is for you! Don't ask yourself, 'Should I buy this book or not?' Go ahead and buy six or seven copies and give them to those you love. You will be investing greatly in their lives."

—**Philip Wagner,** lead pastor of Oasis Church, Los Angeles;
author of *The Marriage Makeover*

"Rick Bezet is the real deal, and he's the perfect person to write a book on how to be real and not fake it. Ever since I've known Rick, he's been a great friend who shares the truth with you and is the same wherever he goes. I highly recommend this book to anyone who is worn out from life and religion or just simply want to live the life God has for you!"

—**Matt Fry,** lead pastor of C3 Church, NC

BE REAL

BECAUSE FAKE
IS EXHAUSTING

RICK BEZET

BakerBooks
a division of Baker Publishing Group
Grand Rapids, Michigan

Published by Baker Books
a division of Baker Publishing Group
P.O. Box 6287, Grand Rapids, MI 49516-6287
www.bakerbooks.com

Paperback ISBN 978-0-8010-1669-1

Printed in the United States of America

The Library of Congress has cataloged the previous edition as follows:
    Bezet, Rick, 1961-
       Be real : because fake is exhausting / Rick Bezet.
          pages cm
       ISBN 978-0-8010-1453-6 (cloth)
       1. Self-perception—Religious aspects—Christianity. 2. Christian life. I. Title.
    BV4598.25.B49 2014
    248.4—dc23   2013036984

Rick Bezet is represented by Thomas J. Winters of Winters, King & Associates, Inc., Tulsa, Oklahoma.

14 15 16 17 18 19 20   7 6 5 4 3 2 1

To the New Life Church family.

Thank you for being all in, for faithfully and sacrificially serving the church, for leading others to Jesus, and for continuing to challenge each other to grow both personally and relationally.

CONTENTS

FOREWORD

For a big portion of my life, I tried to be who I thought others wanted me to be. To my teachers, I was the "good student." To my parents, I was a "good boy." To my college teammates, I was the "good athlete." To my party friends, I was a "good time."

But as hard as I tried to fool others, I wasn't fooling God, and I wasn't fooling myself.

Leadership genius John Maxwell defines success as when those who know you best, love and respect you the most. It was a sobering day when I admitted that those who knew me the least, loved and respected me the most. Those who knew me best . . . well, no one knew the real me but me. No one knew me better than I knew myself. And not only did I not love or respect myself—I couldn't stand myself.

Thankfully, after years of living solely for what others thought, I met the grace of God through Christ in a real and profound way. Instead of trying to live *for* the approval of others, I learned to live *from* the approval of God. And that new life and identity changed everything in my relationships, family, and leadership.

If you haven't noticed, faking it is exhausting. And sadly, our culture is silently training us to do just that. Our friends' lives look more exciting on Instagram and Facebook, so we have to work extra hard to measure up—or at least look like we are.

Recently I read an article that said social media is the newest and biggest driving force of personal discontentment. Everyone else's life looks more fun, more exciting, more fulfilling. While our friends are at the beach, or party, or mall, or ball game, we are stuck in class, or at work, or at home alone. One person summarized the problem by explaining that we are looking at everyone else's "highlight reels" and comparing them to our "behind the scenes." No wonder we feel inadequate. No wonder we put on a show.

Without knowing it, we are becoming consumed with the approval of others. We're infatuated with what others say about us online. We're obsessed with what people think about us. The problem? Becoming obsessed with what others think about us is the quickest way to forget what God thinks about us!

It's time to get real—because being fake is way too exhausting. And that's where Rick Bezet comes in.

I need to be honest with you before I continue: I'm a massive Rick Bezet fan. I love his ministry. I love his family. And I love him as a friend. Why do I love him so much?

Because Rick is the real deal.

The fact that I have to qualify that Rick is the real deal is sad, but we live in a skeptical culture. When we see someone succeeding, many wonder what they are *really* like. Are they the same person behind closed doors as they are in public? Are they really a jerk? Or selfish? Or arrogant? Our skepticism is really just a reflection of our own flaws. The reason we often wonder if others are real is because we know that we're often fake.

The good news is, there is a better way to live. And Rick is the best person I know to lead us on a journey toward personal authenticity and transparency. If you ever interact with Rick in person, you will be struck by his confidence. Don't get me wrong. He isn't cocky in the least. He is simply assured. He knows who he is and would never try to be someone he isn't. Rick is who God made him to be.

That's one of the many reasons so many people love to learn from Rick and benefit greatly from his ministry. As a pastor, teacher, and mentor to thousands, Rick has the unique ability to simultaneously instruct and encourage. His teaching is practical. His stories are inspiring. And his personality is just plain fun.

When you read the words in this book, you'll feel like you're listening to a close friend who loves you and wants the best for you. But let me warn you, Rick won't pull any punches. He's straightforward, direct, and challenging when necessary. And I totally believe God will use Rick's words to empower you to stop faking it and become who God says you are.

So get ready for some gut-wrenching self-examination. Rick will help you discover the powerful truth: You can't please everyone—but you can please God! Instead of living for the approval of people, you can live from the approval of God.

It's time to be real—because fake is exhausting.

Craig Groeschel

ACKNOWLEDGMENTS

Michelle—Thank you for being the kind of wife anybody could be married to. I'm glad I'm the one who is! I couldn't have learned half of what's in this book without you!

Hunter, Hailee, Tanner, and Grace—The greatest kids any parent could have—you don't let me get away with anything! There's not an ounce of fakeness in any of you. Love you!

Joann Bezet (Ms. B.)—There wouldn't even be a New Life Church without you, and you know it, Mom!

Dad, Richard Bezet—Thanks for passing on a great sense of humor! You taught me how to have fun and not take myself too seriously.

Beulah Bezet (Mawmaw B.) and Diane O'Brien—Your prayers made all of this possible. I know you're enjoying being in heaven, but I still think about you every day.

Mike O'Brien—Thank you for raising the best girl on the planet and for showing me how to treat my wife by the way you lived out your marriage with Diane until the last second.

Dudley Delffs—Thank you for all your hard work in putting this book together.

Darren DeLaune, Bobby Hamilton, Harry Bates, Neil Greathouse, Brandon Shatswell, and Jason Kimbrow—Real leadership starts with you guys. New Life Church would not be as healthy without you!

Rachael Bernardi—Your energetic spirit and resourcefulness always kept us on track.

The ARC (Association of Related Churches) leadership team—Thank you for driving the vision of planting relationally healthy churches nationwide. What an amazing ministry and church-planting team God has blessed us with!

Chris and Tammy Hodges and Randy and Amy Bezet—You've always been real, even when I didn't want to hear it! Thank God for best friends like you.

Larry Stockstill—Thanks for being my pastor for so many years. You are such a model to me, and I've learned so much from being around you.

INTRODUCTION

It's Time to Get Real

There is no fear in love. But perfect love drives out fear, because fear has to do with punishment. The one who fears is not made perfect in love.

1 John 4:18

'm usually not a big fan of reality TV shows, but my viewing habits changed a few years ago when one of our church's worship leaders became a finalist on *American Idol*. Kris Allen had always impressed me for two reasons: his incredible vocal talent, which was suddenly being showcased in front of millions of viewers, and his amazing humility and genuine faith. Okay, I guess that's three reasons!

Kris is the real deal, but I'll be honest—I didn't think he would win the entire competition. On the other hand, our worship director, Brandon, told me as soon as he heard Kris was auditioning that Kris would win *American Idol*. Now, none of us doubted Kris's amazing voice, but still we wondered if he could survive the intensity of competing against thousands of other hopeful stars and being criticized by Simon Cowell.

We weren't surprised when Kris passed his audition with flying colors and shouted, "I'm going to Hollywood!" Our church immediately began encouraging, supporting, and praying for Kris. As the weeks went by, he sailed through each round of cuts and made it to the top ten. When the top ten became the final three and Kris was still standing, I started to think twice about Brandon's prophetic words!

His fan base sensed something different about him. It wasn't just his great voice and his ability to fuse different musical styles that appealed to viewers. That same humble spirit and authenticity that we'd seen in Kris for years at our church came through every time he performed. People loved his easygoing personality and natural stage presence. They liked how comfortable and confident he seemed without being cocky. He seemed, well, *real*. And that was a breath of fresh air in an industry where everyone is trying to be flashy and the one with the most stage spunk is the one who takes home the bacon.

Finally, it was down to only three. Before the semifinal, Kris came home, with cameras following his every move, and the towns of Little Rock and Conway—really, the whole state of Arkansas—went nuts. He was a hometown boy hitting the big time, and we were all pumped for him. Kris took it all in stride. He was now a star regardless of the outcome, but he hadn't changed a bit.

For the final performance show, Brandon and I and some others from our church flew out to Hollywood. I've never experienced so much hype, excitement, and sheer adrenaline in one place! Kris was up against Adam Lambert, whose theatrical glam rocker style was sort of a cross between Boy George and KISS. At the beginning of the finale, host Ryan Seacrest summed up the differences between the two perfectly: "the acoustic rocker versus the glam rocker, Conway versus California, the guy next door versus the guyliner."

Even though Kris gave an amazing final performance, I still wasn't sure he could win. Maybe I was afraid for him if he did win. Kris had just gotten married, and I didn't know how a new couple could handle the hype that goes with instant fame and celebrity. Kris was a down-to-earth dude with his feet solidly on the ground—a talented guy with a great voice who just happened to end up competing down to the wire on *American Idol*.

JUST FAKE IT

As you probably know, Kris *did* win! And I couldn't have been happier for him. He handled winning with class and grace, just like he'd handled everything else. And I can testify to the fact that winning hasn't changed Kris one bit. He's still the rock-solid guy who loves his wife, Katy, and proclaims his love for God in the way he lives his life.

It was especially refreshing to see someone as authentic as Kris win and be appreciated for who he is. I think all of us want that kind of acceptance. Maybe not the kind that comes from winning *American Idol*, but the kind of personal confidence that comes from knowing you're fulfilling your destiny, doing exactly what God created you to do. The kind that comes from feeling free to be yourself and not having to worry about what everyone around you thinks. The kind of acceptance that comes from knowing you don't have to be a people pleaser, someone faking it so that others will like you.

Unfortunately, I don't see most people experiencing this kind of freedom to be real—and that ticks me off! Most of us struggle to live up to our full potential and be who God made us to be. We have so many forces pulling us to be what they want us to be instead of who we really are. Our culture today has become jaded and cynical about taking anything, or anyone, at face value.

Politicians are willing to say anything to get a vote. Advertisers will promote anything to maximize profit. Employees will do anything to get ahead, including manipulating data and backstabbing co-workers, and their own bosses may even pressure them to do so. Everywhere we turn we find people wearing masks and faking life to get ahead or just get by.

But being fake not only exhausts us but also takes us even farther away from who we really are and what we truly long for. Despite whatever appearances we work to maintain, we can't fool God. He knows our hearts better than we know them ourselves, including all our secret thoughts, impure desires, and petty emotions.

> **Despite whatever appearances we work to maintain, we can't fool God.**

And he still loves us! He wants us to be real with him. In fact, he *requires* it if we're going to be in relationship with him.

REAL HONESTY

This may sound crazy to you, but I grew up hearing stories like this, so it's normal to me. My friend Thibodeaux was struggling with being honest about who he was—well, maybe it was about how smart he wasn't. Boudreaux and Thibodeaux once were applying for the same job, and the interviewer said, "I can only hire one of you, and whoever scores highest on this test gets the job." After thirty minutes they handed in the test. The interviewer examined them and replied, "You guys scored the exact same on the test. Boudreaux, you get the job." Thibodeaux was furious and demanded to know why his friend got the job if the scores were exactly the same. The interviewer answered, "Because on question number 11, Boudreaux answered, 'I don't know,' and you wrote, 'Me neither.'"

We all say we want to get real, but you can't be real if you're not willing to be honest—totally honest about your struggles, doubts, and failures. God loves it when we approach him this way. He can handle it! If you don't do this, if you're not honest, you'll continue playing games and worrying about what others think of you, and a year from now you could be in the same place you are today. If your desire is to be real, then this book is for you.

Maybe you have come to believe that disguising your feelings and thoughts is the only way to be safe and accepted. It could be that you have become good at faking it. You might even be convinced that it's essential to your success in your relationships, your career, or even your ministry. You've bought into the lie that no one would like, love, or trust you if they really knew who you are and the mistakes you've made. And this lie is killing you. It's stunting your growth and keeping you away from the people you would like to be close to in the first place.

Only a fool looks into the mirror and forgets what he looks like when he goes away (see James 1:23–25 Message). Yet time after time we intentionally walk away and forget because we don't like what we see. And we certainly don't want others to see it. So we've become good at faking it, at creating a mask to cover up the real person we are. Then again, maybe we haven't become so good at it after all! When you stop and think about how many depressed, unhappy, angry, and discontented people you know, you realize maybe we're not fooling anyone by faking it.

> **God accepts us exactly where we are but loves us too much to leave us there.**

Jesus came to bring us the good news that we don't have to fake it. We can be real. God accepts us exactly where we are but loves us too much to leave us there. Can you imagine what your life would be like if you were totally free to be real—all the time? Can you imagine how free you would feel if you could just be yourself and trust others to choose to accept you for who you are? Can you imagine how rested, relaxed, and contented you would be if you didn't have to worry about faking it all the time?

What would it be like if you could walk through life without faking it every day? Can this be done? Can you imagine that it could?

- What if you lived in total honesty with your family?
- What if you had people in your life whom you could tell anything to?
- What if you really believed God loves you no matter what?
- What if you were free to love others like that?
- What if you knew being authentic wouldn't come back to bite you?

This book will give you a map for a better way to live—a more honest and biblical way. The goal is to live a fully integrated life, a life that's stripped of pretense and masks, a life that's uniquely your own and uncommonly real. Not real as our world defines it but real as God, the author of reality, defines it. Living this way doesn't mean that you will be an open book to everyone around you; that would be foolish. But you can learn to live the kind of genuine life that enables you to overcome every fear and false belief and to love others as Christ commands us.

You know there's more to life. It's time to discover the fullness of who you really are and the freedom of living the life God calls you to. If you're tired of settling for less than God's best, then it's time to stop being fake.

If you want to be real, read on.

1

HOW WE LEARNED TO FAKE IT

Coming Clean with Yourself

'm living proof that God has a sense of humor. Considering how much I love being a pastor, it's funny to think about how much I used to hate going to church. My childhood church accidentally taught me many lessons about being real—mostly through negative reinforcement. Fakeness was clearly required before walking through the door, and even though as a kid I couldn't quite put my finger on why, I knew how drained I felt at the end of every service. Church was only an hour and a half long, but it seemed to last the entire Sunday.

The fact that my parents actively played along with the church game didn't help. Their marriage was filled with arguments, disagreements, and more tension than you can imagine. At home, it was like wars and rumors of war! However, when we walked into that church building each week, it was as if a silent switch had been flipped. Our parents gave us kids a look that said, "You'd better play along. Smile, put on the mask, and say all the right things. Do not let anyone know the truth about our family."

And we weren't the only ones. I remember a family that always sat in the same seats in front of us. (Actually, *everyone* sat in the same seats every week.) This family had it all together. I would often find myself wishing that our family was genuinely loving and kind like that family. I wished my parents loved each other like they did. I wished I could have sat still and paid attention like their kids did.

Sadly enough, years later I found out that more terrible things were going on in that home than I thought possible in *any* home: molestation, adultery, physical abuse, bankruptcy, and drug addiction. They were delivering Academy Award–winning performances, because apparently you had to fake it to attend that church. The last thing you ever wanted to do was let anyone know that you were struggling. You had to put on your polite Christian mask, nodding at the right times in the sermon and saying the right things when anyone asked how you were doing.

JOY, JOY, JOY

My Sunday school teacher was no better and seemed to delight in tormenting those of us in her class. As a kid, I hated church and often begged not to go—because of her. I *still* freak out when I think about her! She was the meanest person ever to suck air on the planet and seemed to have it in for me in particular. Even though I was only eight years old, she would tell me, "Bezet, you are going to hell someday." She talked about hell like she was born and raised in hell. She would ask, "Don't you want to go to heaven?" And I would say, "Not if you're going to be there, I don't."

One Sunday she was teaching on the Ten Commandments and mentioned never to take the Lord's name in vain. Without thinking, I blurted out, "Gaw-lee!" She stopped her lesson in midsentence, turned directly to me, and asked very slowly, "What did you just say?" I answered with a quieter "golly" this time. She stared at me with her dark, stone-cold eyes, pointed at me with a knobby finger, and said, "Hell is hot, Bezet! Hell is hot! Hot! HOT!" Can you imagine anyone talking to a child that way and expecting them to discover the joy of the Lord?

In fact, we seemed to sing a lot of songs about joy in that church, but the sour looks on everyone's faces didn't match the words they sang. We'd sing, "I've got the joy, joy, joy, joy down in my heart!"

And everyone shouted, "Where?"

"Down in my heart," they answered.

"Where?"

25

"Down in my heart!"

Asking "Where is our joy?" was the most authentic thing that happened at church. We kept asking but never got a real answer.

THE "GOOD" PASTOR

As a result of my painful church experience growing up, I determined many times that I would never be a fake. As a young adult, I pursued a career as a pro golfer, all the while continuing to search for authentic faith in the one true God. My search was rewarded, and I soon sensed the Lord calling me into full-time—and nonfake—ministry. Some of my youthful enthusiasm and lost hope were restored. That is, until I entered Bible school and discovered that to be a "good pastor," you had to fake it.

Some of the professors and ministry leaders teaching the classes made it clear, directly and indirectly, that as pastors we must always look strong, happy, and in control. No matter what our circumstances or what we are feeling, pastors should always act as though our marriages are happy, our finances are in order, our prayer lives are strong, and we are full of joy! They told us, "If you let people see what's going on inside of you, we will all lose our anointing." Really? Taking their word for it at the time, I bought into a "don't rock the anointing" kind of faith.

But I found myself just as weary, angry, and frustrated as I'd been as a kid in my mean Sunday school teacher's class. I remember thinking, "I can't live this way. I hate living this way! I'm not going to have any friends. I'm going to be lonely and weird, but I will have to fake it and act like I'm *not* lonely and weird for the rest of my life." I would argue back and forth with some of the teachers about this: "Why can't we be real? Why can't we be honest? Why can't we get close to people?" When I would ask these questions, the other students in the room would cringe and look at me like I'd lost my mind. Eventually, they'd just roll their eyes as if to say, "There he goes again."

After hearing the same canned response over and over, I began to take their word for it. I stuffed my feelings and assumed that I just expected too much, that I simply hadn't grown strong enough to display faith in fakeness. Soon I married a woman I loved and started my first year of ministry. Maybe this could work out after all.

"JUST SHUT UP"

I quickly realized it was impossible to minister this way while at the same time struggling in my new marriage with Michelle. We fought all the time. The Bible says don't go to bed with anger in your heart (see Eph. 4:26), so I was staying awake for days at a time! (Okay, that may not be what that verse means.) We felt isolated and secluded because we had no one to talk to or support us. In no time, I became the very thing I swore I would never be: a fake Christian. The results were a bad marriage with no one to tell about it and a ministry that I resented.

During this season of our lives, I was invited to preach at a large church nearby. It was a big deal to me because I had never preached to that many people before. The added stress sent me over the top. Michelle and I had the biggest fight we'd had since we'd been married. She ticked me off, and I yelled back at her, "SHUT UP! JUST SHUT UP!"

She simply stared at me and started crying, but I didn't have time to talk with her about it. I had a sermon to prepare. And I certainly didn't have a friend to call. Meanwhile, Michelle was crying louder and louder in the other room. I felt worse and worse, so I went in there to ask for forgiveness. It took a while, but she forgave me and we made up. I even felt proud of myself for fixing the problem. Then

I went back into the other room to finish my sermon, and that's when I heard the Lord speak to me.

Now, before I tell you what the Lord spoke to me, let me say, I don't hear God very well at times. But this time it was crystal clear. And what he said changed my life. He said, "I forgive you, and so does your wife, but I want you to tell the whole church what you said to her." I remember thinking, "God, I can't do that! You don't know how this works. Lord, you need to go to Bible school! They will clear this up for you *immediately*. This is *not* how you do ministry."

Unsettled by God's message, I decided to change the subject of my sermon. I didn't want to go anywhere near forgiveness or anything that would require transparency on my part. But then—you guessed it—I got up there to preach, and it wasn't working out so well! Nothing made sense. Nobody was responding. Nobody was tracking with me. They just stared at me. I couldn't make a point. I couldn't even finish a sentence. In fact, it was so bad that I finally stopped preaching, turned directly to the people, and said, "This sermon isn't going so well, is it?" It seemed to me like they all answered back simultaneously, "No, it's not!"

At that moment, I started getting real. I closed my Bible and took a deep breath. With Michelle in the front row, I said, "The reason this sermon isn't going so well is because I had a bad day." I then told them about my fight with my wife, hearing the Lord's voice—all the details. I looked at Michelle, and in front of all those people, I sincerely asked her to forgive me. She was shocked, but I felt the anointing of God on me.

You must remember, I had first thought that if I talked this way—that if I opened up and became real and honest—I would be finished for good as a pastor. I honestly thought it would be the last time I'd ever speak in public. *Ever*. I was wrong. In a weird way, I was born again that day. I started over. I thank God for that moment still, and I've kept my promise to him to never turn back to faking it again.

THE REAL THING

It's important for you to realize that being real is not just for Rick Bezet and a few select others. No, it is for you as well. God wants all of us to be real. And as we'll see, he would prefer that we be messed-up people with tender hearts rather than perfect fakers who think they don't need him. God never asked anyone to follow him and be anything other than who he made them to be.

Consider who Jesus, the Son of God, chose to be his closest friends and confidants. It was an earthy, working-class group of fishermen and average joes, not the religious leaders and Jewish elite. He wanted people who were willing to be real, not people who appeared to have it all together. He came for the sick, the broken, the desperate, the hungry, and the heartbroken. The people pretending to have their lives together didn't want to hear what Jesus had to say because they didn't want to be real. They couldn't bear the thought of being just like everyone else—sinners dependent on the love and mercy of God for their lives.

Even though Jesus was godly (God is godly!), the ungodly loved to be around him. And even though he was holy (God is holy!), the unholy wanted to hang out with him!

> God would prefer that we be messed-up people with tender hearts rather than perfect fakers who think they don't need him.

But those who thought they were godly and thought they were holy? They hated him! What's up with that? And did the fishermen and the average joes want to hang out with the ones who only *thought* they were holy? Certainly not.

The early church was known for being a group of people who were real. In Acts 2, Peter preached an extremely bold message, accusing the Jews of being the ones who crucified the Lord. Even where I come from, that's pretty brave! However, something he said caused

29

the Jews to realize he was right, and they responded with the most genuine words: "When the people heard this, they were cut to the heart and said to Peter and the other apostles, 'Brothers, what shall we do?'" (Acts 2:37).

That day three thousand people got saved, and the early church was born. It never would have happened if the Jews had kept to their tradition. They got real, and it changed the world! And this was just the beginning. You can see that the life they lived together was genuine as well:

> Every day they *continued to meet together* in the temple courts. They broke bread *in their homes* and ate together with *glad and sincere hearts*, praising God and *enjoying the favor of all the people*. And the Lord added to their number daily those who were being saved. (Acts 2:46–47, emphasis added)

Look at the words that describe this group: *meeting together, in homes, glad, sincere, praising, enjoying, favor with people*. Imagine that—a growing church with new people being drawn in by the love, sincerity, and gratitude of its members! Isn't this the kind of place where you want to be? It sure is for me, and it's the kind of church I try to lead. My old childhood church didn't act like this. Some in my Bible school didn't teach this. But I made a decision that I wouldn't settle for anything less. And you shouldn't either!

KID STUFF

Maybe you grew up in a church similar to mine and knew something wasn't right. People seemed to be saying and singing one thing and doing and being another. I'm convinced that kids are the very best at recognizing fakeness. They sense when someone is genuine, and even if they can't articulate it, they know when the adults around them are hypocrites.

Because of my passion for being real and helping others be real before God and each other, I pay special attention to the kids in our church. I want them to learn that they can be real and know God. I want them to see genuine faith in action—not just a bunch of talk and phony-baloney. After a recent Sunday service, I was teasing a kid in the church foyer. He was laughing uncontrollably at everything I said. This went on for several minutes. He started pulling on my thumb, so I teased him a little more. I gave him a hard time and he gave me a hard time. Finally, his father came over to get him, and the boy immediately turned and said, "Dad, I just love this man!"

We all cracked up in the moment, but driving home that day, I was struck by the innocence of his comment. He didn't stop to think about whether or not he *should* say it. He didn't think about what he could gain from me by saying it. He didn't calculate how much I'd appreciate and remember him for saying it. He was just in the moment, and he went for it—"Dad, I just love this man!" This kid is young, he's innocent, and he's real!

Being real is natural for kids, and they notice when adults are real and when they're faking it. When we grow older, however, and especially after we've been a Christian for a long time, we tend to begin to cultivate a mask. I'm sorry to say that many people, instead of becoming more welcoming and more concerned for others, drift to a style of Christianity that few could find attractive. Fake becomes their default setting. Real becomes something that seems too scary, too vulnerable, too unnerving. The result may be that we lose our childlike faith.

Maybe at this point you think I'm being too tough on people who fake it. Perhaps you think that Jesus wouldn't feel this way. If you believe that is true, then I would ask you to reconsider the New Testament, particularly the conversations Jesus had with religious leaders of the day.

Jesus spent a lot of his time pointing out the fakeness of the Pharisees and scholars around him. He repeatedly and consistently used

They became so concerned with being better than everyone else that they forgot how to be real.

harsh language and bold, direct confrontations to get their attention. Check out Matthew 23, an entire chapter of dialogue Jesus directed at the Pharisees and other religious leaders. After you read it, you may actually think I'm too mild in my approach!

Now Jesus turned to address his disciples, along with the crowd that had gathered with them. "The religion scholars and Pharisees are competent teachers in God's Law. You won't go wrong in following their teachings on Moses. But be careful about following them. *They talk a good line, but they don't live it.* They don't take it into their hearts and live it out in their behavior. *It's all spit-and-polish veneer."* (Matthew 23:1–3 Message, emphasis added)

I suspect many of these same people started out sincere but got caught up in the politics and fakeness that can easily invade our religious culture. They became so concerned with being better than everyone else that they forgot how to be real.

TELL THE TRUTH

How about you—do you feel like you're able to be real about who you are and what you struggle with? Do you feel like you've made many mistakes in life? Big mistakes? Some people who think they are perfect may say, "Not many." Let me just say right here, if you think you're perfect, then most people probably don't like being around you. *You* may not even like being around you. If you don't think you have an issue, that is your issue!

Consider this: it's tough to be married to someone who thinks they're perfect. Or work with them. Or do business with them. Or be their friend. That's because people who think they're perfect are constantly working to prove that—to themselves and everybody else. But it takes a lot of energy to do that. At the end of the day, they're exhausted, and they don't even know why, because in the process of deceiving everybody else, the person they've most successfully deceived is themselves. Deep down, we all know we're not perfect, but in order to sustain the pretense, we have to master the art of deception.

Let me ask you: Have you ever lied before? A big fat lie? No? How about trying to make an impression on someone that was anything other than the naked truth? Any form of intentional deception is lying! If you're still saying no, there's a good chance you're lying to yourself right now. You might want to stop and think about why you picked up this book in the first place!

Here's another question: Have you ever stolen something? Oh, nothing? Not even an ink pen or supplies from your workplace? Have you ever borrowed something, like a book, meaning to give it back, but you know good and well it's still sitting on your shelf? What about when you were a kid? It all counts!

Have you ever found yourself taking God out of the center of your life and replacing him with money, success, a new boat, a better neighborhood, a promotion at work?

Do you ever procrastinate? (You may need to think about the answer to that one and get back to me sometime.)

Let's stop and think for a moment. You just admitted that you're a liar, a thief, and an idolater, and eventually you may even admit to being a procrastinator. A great way to begin a book on being real, don't you think?

I promise you this—I'm right there beside you. I've made plenty of mistakes in my life and will admit many of them throughout the pages that follow. I'll tell you some of the mistakes I've made in my marriage (besides telling Michelle to shut up!) as well as ways I've failed as a parent. In fact, what my wife and I have learned about parenting is that even when you have the best of intentions, you still fail.

For instance, when our son was six years old, he was going around telling everyone at church that he was the pastor's son. He did this because, evidently, he was able to get extra cookies in children's church. When my wife found out he was doing this, she told him, "No, son, this is not the way we roll. You don't go around telling people you are the pastor's son in order to get something extra. You just tell people you're Tanner. That's good enough. Do you hear me?" He responded, "Yes ma'am!"

The next Sunday, a lady in the church asked him, "Aren't you the pastor's son?" Tanner thought about his dilemma for a minute, then said, "Well, I *thought* I was, but my mom said I'm *not*." (Tell me that won't stunt the growth of a church!) Talk about context making a difference in how the truth is told! This wasn't exactly a great way to impress visitors.

DRIFTING

Unlike my son, most of us know too well when we're putting a spin on the truth. We deliberately try to arrange the truth, or at least part of it, in a way that will make us look as good as possible. We may start out with good intentions but wind up bending the truth to protect ourselves or to get what we're after. A little white lie here, a little half-truth there, and soon it's a way of life. When we fake our way through life, we start out moving toward God but find ourselves drifting away. It's a subtle shift that carries us farther and farther away from our original intention of being real.

Have you ever drifted on the water on a lazy summer afternoon? There's nothing like it for a relaxing way to soak up the sun. Our family loves going on vacation to the beach. Ever since our kids were young, one of our favorite places to go has been the Florida coast, especially Destin. One thing we love to do is to get on our rafts, floats, and boogie boards and ride the waves together.

One time many years ago, we were all out there, floating on the water, doing what Bezets do. After about thirty minutes or so, we looked back to the shore to find our chairs and umbrella, but we couldn't see them. Nothing looked the same—not only could I not find our stuff on the beach, but I didn't even see our condo. It was as if we had been plopped down on the shore of some alien planet where everything was sort of familiar but unrecognizable. We had drifted! Without us realizing it, while we were just playing in the water, the current caused us to end up in a place we didn't expect.

> **When we fake our way through life, we start out moving toward God but find ourselves drifting away.**

Drifting happens to everyone at some point. And without being anchored to the solid foundation of a genuine relationship with God, we'll continue to be tossed around like a piece of driftwood. Even the first couple on the planet had to deal with ending up in a place they didn't plan to be. Adam and Eve started out in the right place, but they drifted too. When they met, Adam was blown away by Eve's beauty, and they fell in love. They had it made! Adam was never late coming home from work. Eve never burnt any dinners. He was the most handsome man in the world, and she was the most beautiful woman. There were no marriage problems and no kids throwing fits. There were also no bills to pay and no shopping malls. Perfect! And there were no in-laws and no clothes either. Like I said, they had it made!

You may know the end of Adam and Eve's story. The Bible says they were full of shame and fear. In Genesis 3:10, Adam says to God, "I heard you in the garden, and I was afraid because I was naked; so I hid."

They blew it, and then they did what comes naturally when people know they have sinned: they hid. And after that, they started faking it. They became embarrassed and ashamed, and they tried covering it all up instead of being real with God about what was going on. They went from walking with God in the cool of the evening to hiding and blaming each other. They went from the innocence of being naked and unashamed to crouching behind fig leaves to hide the bare-naked truth of their disobedience against God.

COMING CLEAN

Like our original parents, Adam and Eve, somewhere along the way we lost our ability to be totally real. It may be more complicated and our fig leaves may have designer labels on them, but we're still doing the same basic thing today. We're hiding. We're lying. We're covering up the truth. We're not being real.

But, my friend, we don't have to live this way! Jesus paid a huge price for you to come out of hiding and walk in the cool of the evening with him again. When we cling to behaviors like shame, fakeness, hiding, and blaming others, it's only because we forget what we have in the gift of Christ.

On the one hand, we know that we have him, including all access to the Father and his loving-kindness and mercy. But on the other hand, we act like Adam and Eve, who lost all innocence and were forced out of the Garden. They had no idea of the atonement that would soon be available to them.

But Jesus has reopened the door to intimacy with God. We don't have to stay trapped in our own efforts and shameful cover-ups. Because of Christ, now we're only trapped when we don't allow God access to our lives. Hebrews 10:22 tells us, "Draw near to God with a sincere heart." When we draw near to him—when we get real with God—he draws close to us and holds us as his beloved children.

And guess what? In the process of becoming real, not only does God draw us close to him, but he also pulls friends around us who can be there for us as well. I have a lot of great friends who speak truth into my life at different levels. But two of them—Chris Hodges and my brother, Randy Bezet—I simply can't do without. They check on me and I check on them. We're honest with each other about what's going on in our lives. These two know me so well that when I walk in the room, they know if I am off my game, and they call me out if they have to. I'll talk more about how crucial it is to have friends later in the book, but I want you to know up front how important this is to me.

Maybe you also started out right and then somehow ended up in a place where you are now faking it. My hope is that reading this book can be a turning point for you. That you'll do some honest soul searching. That you won't feel your life is so fragmented by trying to be all things to all people and losing yourself in the process.

As you continue to give God more room in the mix of your life, you'll discover that living in freedom from fear in your relationships is much more fun than being addicted to the approval of others. You'll find courage that you didn't even know you had as you relate to others right where you are (and right where *they* are). You'll break the vicious cycle of hiding, being exposed, then hiding again. God made you to be real and to be free. That's what I'm talking about!

2

WRESTLING TO BE REAL

I Won't Let Go until You Bless Me

Something really unusual happened to me after a weekend service about five years ago. It happened to be a weekend when I didn't preach, and I was there to enjoy the service and hang out with people. After the service, as I was standing around talking with friends, a distinguished-looking man approached me. He looked as though he had been crying, and his wife and two children were standing in single file right behind him, all with very serious looks on their faces.

Without even telling me his name, this man told me that he had physically pushed his wife hard last night, in the presence of their kids. That certainly explained the tense expressions and downcast eyes from each member of his family. Shaking uncontrollably, the man lowered his voice to almost a whisper as he asked, "Would you allow a man like me to come to this church?"

For one of the few times in my life, I was speechless. I looked at him for a moment and then saw his wife behind him staring very hard at me as if to say, "You'd *better* say yes." And of course I did.

In the weeks that followed, I saw this family get involved in our church like no other I've witnessed. Slowly they began to experience God's healing in their lives, their marriage, and their family. To this day, they still serve in our church each week with huge smiles on their faces. The wife has thanked me a couple of times for that moment after the service.

RUNNING OR WRESTLING

The truth is that I simply did what any decent pastor—or honest Christian—would do. It was the man who decided to be honest and real who turned that family around. His courage illustrates something I've observed over the years: real change usually happens as a result of an uncomfortable, even painful situation—one that causes you to get real before God because nothing else will work!

We see this turning point in so many biblical stories but perhaps nowhere more clearly than in the life of a man known for his chronic deception. Toward the beginning of the Bible we meet a strong-willed child named Jacob. How do we know he was strong willed? The Bible says he and his brother, Esau, were duking it out in the womb (see Gen. 25:22)! How do you even do that? How do you fight with your brother before you're born? I don't know exactly, but the Bible says that when Esau was born first, Jacob was hanging on to Esau's ankle as he came out of the womb (see Gen. 25:26).

> **Real change usually happens as a result of an uncomfortable, even painful situation.**

Jacob was the second born. In Jewish culture, the inheritance, the favor, and the blessing always went to the firstborn. That ticked Jacob off—he thought he deserved his dad's inheritance. And he wasn't the only one. The Bible shows that Jacob's mom, Rebekah, coddled and spoiled him to the point that he felt entitled to take matters into his own hands. He became a trickster, a world-class con artist.

With his mother's prodding, Jacob schemed to manipulate his dad and steal his brother's inheritance. And it worked—to a degree. He got what he wanted, but at what price? Lying and deceiving his poor, old, blind father? Enraging and estranging his twin brother? Jacob was always fighting for things, but even when he got what he thought he wanted, his life kept spinning out of control. Even his honeymoon night was weird at best—he woke up married to the wrong woman! You can't make this stuff up. Jacob was a mess, and his relationship with his brother was a huge mess.

But he wasn't without hope. Somehow in the midst of his mess, he knew that God had not given up on him. It's very interesting that right before Jacob and Esau saw each other again for the first time in twenty years, something unusual happened. Jacob was so scared of confrontation with Esau that he sent his wife and children ahead and went to be alone. But God seized that moment to do something unique. Consequently, in Genesis 32, we read about an unusual wrestling match:

> Jacob was left alone, and a man wrestled with him till daybreak. When the man saw that he could not overpower him, he touched the socket of Jacob's hip so that his hip was wrenched as he wrestled with the man. Then the man said, "Let me go, for it is daybreak."
> But Jacob replied, "I will not let you go unless you bless me."
> The man asked him, "What is your name?"
> "Jacob," he answered.
> Then the man said, "Your name will no longer be Jacob, but Israel, because you have struggled with God and with humans and have overcome."
> Jacob said, "Please tell me your name."
> But he replied, "Why do you ask my name?" Then he blessed him there.
> So Jacob called the place Peniel, saying, "It is because I saw God face to face, and yet my life was spared." (vv. 24–30)

Change often begins with discomfort or an issue of some sort or another. And it may not be something sudden. In fact, it may be something that has been there for a while but surfaces in a moment of tension. Most of our problems don't happen overnight. That's been my experience.

Not long ago my phone rang in the middle of the night. I fumbled around to find it and finally answered. "Hello?"

"Hey, Pastor Rick. We've got a serious problem! Things are messed up, man!"

"What is it?" I asked. I'm used to being called when tragedy strikes.

"It's my marriage, man. It's bad!" He choked up with emotion.

"Well," I asked him, "what's going on? How long has it been messed up?"

"From the very beginning—about twenty-three years!"

I looked at the phone and said, "Come on, dude! Your marriage has been in trouble for that many years and you're calling me in the middle of the night? Can't it wait till morning? Now hang up and get some sleep!"

But that's exactly how we are! We get to our breaking point and then want a magic pill to cure our problem. We realize we don't have God, and suddenly we're desperate for his help. Sometimes this is where we need to be—right in the middle of a crisis where we need God more than anything else. God often does his best work when we're hemmed in with nowhere else to turn.

CRY UNCLE

When we have exhausted ourselves by trying to change under our own power, we often find ourselves wrestling with God, just like Jacob. Some people want to debate who Jacob was wrestling with, but the Bible clearly tells us. Hosea 12:3 says, "Even in the womb, Jacob struggled with his brother; when he became a man, he even fought with God" (NLT). I'm convinced that this does not mean we have to fight God, though. We simply have to get out of the way and stop resisting what he would like to do in our lives. In other words, your biggest conflict is when you're fighting against what God is trying to do in your life.

If you go to play a pickup basketball game and LeBron James happens to be there, and he's on your team, let me give you a little advice: *Don't hog the ball!* Give the ball to LeBron! He's really, really good. Get out of his way and let him do what he's good at!

In the same way, we have to remember that God is also really, *really* good! The Bible says he can palm the universe with his hand (see Isa. 40:12). But instead of passing to him for the easy shot, we hog the ball! We try to take all the shots, we try to do everything, and then when a crisis comes, we try to fix it. If we'll only stop and listen, we'll hear God saying, "Let me have a shot at it. I've got some pretty good stats. Check this out." But we say, "No, no, no. I want to take another shot! I'm the star here!"

It's a pride thing, and you can see it in Jacob. When they were wrestling, Jacob refused to be beaten. He had spent his whole life figuring out how to con, lie, deceive, and spin things the way he wanted them. Only now he had met his match—someone who wasn't going to let him get away with his usual nonsense. Someone who knew Jacob better than he knew himself.

The object of most wrestling matches is to pin the other guy so he'll cry uncle and give up. But when you're wrestling with God, you can't win—at least not the way we typically think about winning. God doesn't want to defeat us. He wants to wake us up to what he can do in us. When you resist God, like Jacob did, you're really not fighting him as much as you're fighting yourself.

BATTLE FOR A BLESSING

The Bible says Jacob couldn't win the match. And certainly God could have wrapped it all up immediately. But the Lord was looking for something. I have said many times that God loves you just the way you are, and that's true. He does! But he also loves you *far too much to let you stay that way*. He wants you to put him first and live a holy and clean life. He wants to change you. He wants to help you to grow, to be better, to be different, to be all you were meant to be.

And so he allows a crisis. He allows you to make your own choices and do things your own way. Why? Because we rarely change until the pain exceeds our fear of change. We don't change when we see the light. We change when we feel the heat.

When the heat is on, you've got to do something. You can either give up, do something stupid, or hold on to God with all your might.

If we grab hold of God, we refuse to give in to despair. We stay committed to the solution. We realize we can't win doing life our way, so we're finally ready to turn desperation into devotion. We won't let go of God's potential. We say, "I'm sticking with this until God shows me the way!" That's what Jacob did. We're told, "Then the man said, 'Let me go, for it is daybreak.' But Jacob replied, 'I will not let you go unless you bless me'" (Gen. 32:26). He knew that if he gave up, he'd miss the blessing.

> We don't change when we see the light. We change when we feel the heat.

See, here's the problem: many of us aren't pursuing a relationship with God. We expect him to give us what we want, but we don't want to know him on his terms. So instead of turning to him, we keep trying to do things our way.

As a result, many of us are dry and weary. We really don't have anything fresh happening inside of us, and we're moving through life with a lot of ambition, a lot of goals. I am amazed at the behavior patterns of some of the people who attend our church—the aggressiveness of the goals they have and the way they pursue everything. They get up early and they work late. They're going for it! But the fact of the matter is, there's not much room for the Lord.

As Jacob struggled with God, he was *still* trying aggressive behavior—only this time his goal, his pursuit, was to get the blessing! This is right where you need to be. God is looking for somebody who says, "I'm gonna keep hanging on to you, God, until you bless me, until you're a part of my life."

Why did God let the struggle go on? Here's the lesson: when God allows a crisis into your life, sometimes he doesn't solve it immediately.

He lets it continue for a while. Why? I believe he wants to see if you really mean business, if you are really ready to accept his solution, if you really want to get something out of it. Is it a desperate, childish whim, or is it a real, deep desire?

God is looking for the committed—people who will keep their focus, their gaze, their attention on him no matter what! People who won't give up the fight until they find the blessing. Aggressive? Yes! Only in a new direction: God's direction. Jacob was no longer aggressive toward his personal goals and ambitious pursuits. He was aggressive toward God!

WHO DO YOU THINK YOU ARE?

Notice what happened next in Jacob's wrestling match with God: "The man asked him, 'What is your name?'" (Gen. 32:27). Now, this is a very strange question since obviously God already knew Jacob's name!

Why bother to ask Jacob his name? In ancient cultures, you were always named for your character. Your name was a brand or a label based on your essence, the kind of person you were. So what God was really asking Jacob was, "What is your character? Who are you? At the core of your heart, what are you about?" God knew that Jacob needed to own up to who he was. It was time for old Jake to come clean, admitting the truth to himself and to God.

When Jacob said, "My name is Jacob," he was really saying, "Okay, I'll tell you what's going on. I'll tell you who I am. *I'm a deceiver.* I've been a liar my whole life. I'm a manipulator." He was admitting it. He'd ripped off everybody. He'd lied to his brother. He'd made a grab for his brother's inheritance. He'd lied to his dad, who was going blind. He'd cheated his brother out of his rightful blessing. He'd used his father-in-law. He'd used his wife—or should I say *wives*? He was one big manipulator. He was a fighter against the truth. *Jacob.*

Talk about humbling! If you were named for your greatest character flaw, what would you be called? "Hi, I'm Greedy." Or would it be Bitter? Angry? Uncontrollable Temper? Lustful? A User? "Hi, I'm Depressed . . . I'm Fearful . . . I'm Afraid . . . I'm Gossip . . ."

This is where it all starts coming together. You're in the match. God's got you pinned down. But you have to give him something to work with. What is it that's wrong with your life? Who have you been so far, based on your character, your actions and decisions? To encounter God, to get to the point where you actually have a relationship with God, you've got to get honest about what's going on. Because when you get honest, he changes you.

NO LONGER SECRET IDENTITY

As a result of his honesty and his unwillingness to give up the good fight, Jacob got a new name—and along with it, a new identity. "Then the man said, 'Your name will no longer be Jacob, but Israel, because you have struggled with God and with humans and have overcome'" (Gen. 32:28). God said to him, "All right, since you've been honest with me and you've admitted who you are, I'm going to give you a new name, a new identity."

God knew everything about Jacob—every lie, every deception, every *thought* of lying—and yet he still knew that was not who Jacob really was. God knew there was more to Jacob because he had created him.

No matter how messed up you are, God can turn your life around. God knew Jacob's name. And God knows your name. He knows your weaknesses, and he knows your strengths. He knows who you think you are and who you really are.

But you've got to give God something to work with—a ground zero foundation of honesty. You and I will never be able to change until we openly, honestly, and authentically admit our sin, our weaknesses, and our character defects to ourselves, to God, and to other people.

If you're exhausted by your own failed efforts to change, and if you're unwilling to give up until you get the blessing, come clean. Stop making excuses. Stop rationalizing. Stop justifying. Stop blaming other people. Come to God and say, "God, I want to own up to the weaknesses, the filth, the dishonesty, the wrong in my life." When you come and tell God, "This is who I really am," he's not going to be surprised.

> **No matter how messed up you are, God can turn your life around.**

You might be a liar. You might need to say, "I'm addicted to pornography." You might have a serious anger problem and be tired of hurting people. It could be that you have secret shame or a past nobody knows about.

God is saying, "Hey, who are you? Tell me, so I can change you! But you have to start with the truth about who you are. You have to admit it."

What do you need to admit about yourself? When are you going to face the truth about yourself? Fill in the blank: "I am a _____." Is this just to make you grovel and feel bad about yourself? No! It's so you can tell yourself the truth (remember, God already knows!) and face the light. God loves you too much to leave you where you are, but you have to see it yourself if you're ever going to move on from it.

NEW NAME

When Jacob got real with God, he got a brand-new identity. God said, "Your name was Jacob—the manipulator. That's the old you. We're not going to call you that anymore. We're going to change your name. We're going to call you Israel." This new name means "Prince with God." Think about it: to wrestle with someone, you have to be hanging on. You have to be engaged intensely. God said, "I

> **When we know who we truly are, it's not so hard to be real.**

know you've blown it, I know you're conniving, but I see something else in you. Beneath all your deceit, striving, and competitiveness, all the stuff you don't want anybody else to know about, I see someone who hangs on for my blessing."

Jacob wasn't the only one in the Bible to get a divine name change. God often changed people's names: from Abram to Abraham, from Sarai to Sarah, from Simon to Peter, from Saul to Paul. He loves to reveal to his children who they really are—not who they've been or who they think they are.

When we know who we truly are, it's not so hard to be real.

LEADING WITH A LIMP

Once Jacob got a new identity, he got blessed. Look at God's loving and gracious response to Jacob's confession: "Jacob said, 'Please tell me your name.' But he replied, 'Why do you ask my name?' Then he blessed him there. So Jacob called the place Peniel, saying, 'It is because I saw God face to face, and yet my life was spared'" (Gen. 32:29–30). God always blesses you when you encounter him.

God also gave Jacob a reminder of his experience. This was the turning point of Jacob's life, and God didn't want him to ever forget it! So in the struggle, God dislocated Jacob's hip and left a weakness (see Gen. 32:31). For the rest of his life, Jacob walked with a limp.

What's the significance of this limp? It stopped Jacob's lifelong pattern of running. If you know anything about Jacob's life, you know he was constantly creating trouble and running from it. But

God said, "I can stop that. I'll give you a limp. You'll never run away from life again." The reminder of his encounter with God was that he would never walk the same again.

It is never God's will for you to run from a problem. *Never.* If you run from it, it will just come up again, because God is more interested in changing your character than in making your life comfortable. When you have an encounter with God, when you really meet God, it changes the way you walk. You cannot meet somebody who is as great as God and not have your desires change.

When you see yourself the way God sees you, it's going to change your life.

This may be the most important thing I tell you: the deepest work God does in your life is when he works on your identity. When you see yourself the way God sees you, it's going to change your life. You'll be set free from the old you, and you can start acting in a whole new way.

Everyone who encountered Jesus experienced this kind of transformation. For example, Jesus said to the woman caught in adultery, "Go now and leave your life of sin" (John 8:11). His power set her free. The apostle Paul says in 2 Corinthians 5:17, "If anyone is in Christ, he is a new creation; old things have passed away; behold, all things have become new" (NKJV).

The new walk that God wants to give you will change you for good. *Forever.* But you have to have an honest encounter with God. Pursue him! Don't let go of him! In the midst of the crisis, be willing to admit to God who you really are. That's what he's looking for: honesty and a willingness to change. He'll do a new thing. He'll give you a new strength. He'll give you a new identity, and he'll give you a new walk. It's not just for the Jacobs and Sauls and people who seriously mess up. It's for all of us—for you and for me! If we'll go for God and have encounters with him, we'll walk differently for the rest of our lives, and nobody can take that from us.

Jacob's limp was a daily reminder to depend on God. The thigh muscle is the largest and strongest muscle in the body. God touched Jacob at his greatest point of strength and created a weakness out of it. From that point on, Jacob was going to have to stand in God's power, not his own. Jacob left this situation both stronger and weaker—stronger because he was not the same person anymore; there'd been a conversion, a change, a transformation. All the junk in his past had been dealt with. But he was also weaker because he was going to have to depend on God for his daily walk. We too have to remember to depend on God's strength and not our own.

DON'T LET GO!

One of our best reminders of God's power in our lives is the cross. I love having the symbol of the cross in our church. But when you look at it, it's really just a piece of wood. It represents something powerful, but it's really nothing unless you've had an encounter with God at the cross.

Similarly, we can't just have the liturgy at church. We have to have an experience with God. We have to let him change us, often by letting him take our greatest point of strength to a place of true vulnerability. The point where we have to rely on him alone, not ourselves. Every day. Every hour. Every moment. *Now.*

I know this kind of reliance on God is easier said than done. Years ago I was asked to officiate a wedding ceremony, and the families asked if my son, who was four at the time, could be in it as well. Despite a raised-eyebrow look from my wife, I said, "Sure!"

Then the bride's mother or the wedding planner or someone had the strange—I mean, *unique* (in case she's reading this!)—idea to have my son bring in a big Bible and hand it to me at the beginning of the service. We went through the rehearsal and everything seemed to be going great. It was the first time I had seen my son up on the stage in front of a lot of people, and he seemed very confident. At the same time, I was still a little nervous. You never know what a kid is going to do at a wedding.

The next day, the day of the wedding, my son started acting weird. He was being really quiet, and when I asked him how he was doing, he just sort of nodded and shrugged awkwardly.

I said, "Son, are you okay?"

He said, "Dad, call those people and tell them I don't want to be in the wedding."

"What's wrong?" I asked.

He looked at me and said, "Dad, I'm gonna mess it up. I just know it!" And he crumpled on the spot.

I thought for a moment and said, "Son, I'm willing to make that phone call, but I have an idea that'll give you some confidence for what you're supposed to do in the wedding." I could tell I had his attention, so I kept going. "This is all you have to do. They're going to open the doors in the back of the church, and when they open the doors, all you've got to do is keep your eyes on your father and carry the Bible. That's all you've got to do. That's really the only thing they want you to do. If you keep your eyes on me and carry the Word, we'll get through this." I prayed for him, and he agreed to go for it.

When the service started, he was back there looking up at me with all his might. He stared straight ahead at me, and nothing could take his eyes off me. He wasn't even blinking! I looked at his knuckles, and he was carrying the Bible so tightly that there was no way anybody could get that Bible out of his hands! He started walking, holding on to God's Word and looking ahead to where his father was leading him. He didn't look back. He didn't let go. He marched right up front and handed me that Bible.

If we're willing to do the same thing, we can accomplish more than we've ever imagined. Sometimes you are broken down, and you just want to quit. You just want to bail out. You don't want to do it anymore. But if you can remember on those days to keep your eyes on your Father and carry the Word, it'll always get you to another step. It'll make you stronger. "He gives strength to the weary and increases the power of the weak. Even youths grow tired and weary, and young men stumble and fall; but those who hope in the LORD will renew their strength. They will soar on wings like eagles; they will run and not grow weary, they will walk and not be faint" (Isa. 40:29–31).

A lot of times we want to lie and manipulate. We want God to do his part, but we don't want to contribute. Listen, you have to give God something to work with. You have to be real. This is what it's all about. Don't look back, and don't let go!

3

DONE WITH DOING LIFE ALONE

Being Real Requires Community

ave you ever seen the History channel's reality show *Swamp People*? Ever notice how people on that show act and sound a little different than your average American? Now, don't get me wrong. I'm not being disrespectful to Cajuns—after all, I *am* one! We Cajuns spend a lot of time catching fish, crawfish, gators, and snakes in the bayous, the small waterways that fill southern Louisiana. I eat ditch food—and love it! To me, there's nothing better than a crawfish boil and boudin sausage.

But until *Swamp People* came along, Cajuns had historically been more isolated from America than most groups—to the point where, when you watch that show, you might have to strain a bit to understand them. And their actions, their behavior patterns, are a little bit different from what you may be used to. They don't always do things quite like most folks do.

Take my Cajun friend Boudreaux, for example. He was really hungry one day, but he got turned around downtown. True to form, he didn't notice where he was, and he walked up to the counter and said, "I want two cheeseburgers, a fry, and a Coke."

The lady said, "What?"

Thinking she didn't hear him, Boudreaux shouted, "I said I want two cheeseburgers, a fry, and a Coke!"

The lady gently responded, "Sir, this is a *library*!"

Boudreaux looked at her, puzzled, then whispered, "I want two cheeseburgers, a fry, and a Coke."

Sometimes when I'm preaching or joking around with friends, I refer to a fictitious place nearby called Bayou Self. It's the worst place to live—Bayou Self (by-your-self)—because there's nobody around, and you start thinking and acting a little differently than everybody else. Too much time in Bayou Self may drive you a little crazy!

ISO-LOCATIONS

You don't have to be in the bayou to experience the lonely separation that comes from creating an "iso-location." I'm guessing we're all prone to it and even take it for granted. Many times I've heard somebody say, "You can tell what a person is really like when they're all alone." Really? As if we have to be isolated to really understand who we are?

The more I heard this, the more I realized I know *exactly* what we all look like when we're all alone. You see, we all look *the same* when we're alone. Lonely. Anxious. Maybe a little scared. A little bit crazy. Not healthy. Nothing to listen to but the little voices in our head.

Have you ever seen a weird Christian? You know, that person who has that faraway look in their eyes and always talks about what

We were made to live in community with others.

God told them to do that day? Something like, "God told me to eat Frosted Flakes instead of Froot Loops this morning." I want to tell them that maybe they have eaten a few too many Froot Loops, if you know what I mean. It always seems clear to me that these Froot Loopers have been spending way too much time by themselves.

Solitary confinement is also said to be the worst form of punishment in the prison system. I believe it! We were not made to live alone. We were made to live in community with others.

I thank God all the time for the Association of Related Churches and the relationships I share with other ARC pastors as we walk through ministry together, checking on one another and praying for one another. Some of the weirdest people I know are pastors who are all alone, living on an island, with nobody telling them what's going on. If you look in the mirror and you see something hanging out of your nose, you know everybody else sees it too! But people won't tell you what you need to hear if you don't give them permission, although they will talk about it when you're not around. The ARC is a bunch of people in ministry who talk about things together. We bring up the blind spots, the weaknesses that we deal with in ourselves. We care. It's a group of people who, I believe, operate the way God originally wanted the church to function. I thank God I'm involved with that.

God even said, while he was setting up creation, "It is not good for the man to be alone" (Gen. 2:18). This verse is generally used to make the point that Adam needed a helper, in the form of a wife, which is true. But children, and more children, and eventually generations of children, and families that became tribes—all people in community with one another—was where God was going with all of this! Adam was not made by God to live alone. And you're not made to live alone either.

Isolation is not the plan God has for his people. People hide for many reasons. We already saw that Adam and Eve were hiding from God, as if that were going to work. On a planet with over seven billion people, we might be tempted to think that we can get lost in the crowd and hide from God for a while. But whether we're one of two, like Adam and Eve, or one of two gazillion, ultimately we can't hide from God—or ourselves. You see, when we hide, it's mostly because we feel ashamed.

TWO ROADS

Several years ago I got a call telling me that a pastor friend of mine, who had been a mentor to me, had fallen into sin. I was shocked. How did my friend, who seemed to love God even more than I did, get to this place? How did it happen? After some conversations, I discovered it was simple. He was doing life alone!

If we don't stay connected to real, honest-to-goodness, transparent community, we usually go down one of two roads. The first road leads to a feeling of rejection. We close our hearts and build walls because somebody hurt us and we were offended. We may keep smiling and praying and even preaching and teaching, but we decide we're not going to let anyone hurt us again. Through it all, we end up saying, "I'm never going to be close to anyone again so I won't get hurt again."

The problem with this defensive strategy is that it will ultimately kill you. Ironically enough, the people who offended you keep on hurting you when you're walled in to isolation! Sometimes we try to justify our lone ranger mind-set by Christianizing it with Scripture. We may say, "All I need is God. That's really all I need. I just need the Lord." But I dare you to show me one verse

God alone is not all you need.

in the Bible that says that all you need is God. God didn't design us that way! We've already covered the fact that God made us to live in community with him and each other. God alone is not all you need.

The second road leads to a more aggressive response, even to the point of acting out. If we're doing this, then we are also isolating inwardly, but it just shows up in a more obvious way. After all, we're lonely and hurting, so we deserve a little comfort, right? And since we're not being honest and transparent with others, no one has to know.

Before you know it, unhealthy patterns develop, secret sins persist, and silent addictions may even take root. Soon we feel too ashamed, or maybe too proud, to even admit our failures and temptations to somebody else. In fact, we're convinced that if we mention a temptation to a friend, we'll be gossiped about or, if we're in ministry, even lose our job for being tempted. Sadly enough, that is sometimes the case. But temptation isn't sin—it's just sin knocking on our door! Temptation doesn't become sin until we give in and let the temptation blossom into disobedience. It's no coincidence that our enemy knows that one of the best ways to combat temptation is to be connected with friends. Confessing what you're going through takes the sting out of the enemy's bite.

SOCIAL MEDIOCRITY

Another reason we don't typically have connected relationships is the pace of life. We're all going for self-fulfillment. Individualism and personal goals are raging out of control, and we're traveling through life at a high rate of speed. It's really hard to establish and build enduring relationships when we're moving through life at a Mach 2 pace.

Today's technology may not be helping us stay connected either. We think we are so connected through Facebook, Twitter, YouTube, Instagram, and Pinterest. (What's Pinterest all about anyway?) My point is this: these connections we're making through social media are increasingly superficial. They're not contributing to real community and personal connection—they're thwarting it. On Twitter, we're forced to limit the content of our communication to 140 characters. On Facebook, we control what we post and manipulate our status, photos, and "Likes" so that others will envy us, admire us, and like us back. The unwritten goal of Facebook is for you to put your best face out there. Maybe we should call it Fakebook.

And it's not just in our country or one particular culture that we see the impact of social media. You can travel all over the world and see people texting. I was in Africa a while back, and you could be riding an elephant in the middle of nowhere, sending an Instagram. It's just crazy how fast information travels these days. And now, as the technology is accepted and used more and more, some of us think that our true friends are the people on Facebook rather than those we have real relational connections with!

An increasingly common phenomenon is when a woman gets on Facebook, sees an old boyfriend, starts talking with him, and in a matter of minutes he's saying, "Wow, you're still pretty! You look good! You look just like you did in high school." Before her husband knows it, she's packed her bags and left for a fairy tale, a teenaged fantasy of days gone by, a fake relationship. She forgets that this guy on Facebook is *lying* to her (why did she break up with him in the first place?)! Besides, he's probably got a mullet anyway!

Unfortunately, we've gotten used to shallow relationships. Social media has become social mediocrity. We then get knocked off track because we don't even know what's real anymore. It just seems like the more technologically connected we get in this age, the less connected we really are. So we are actually becoming *more* isolated, even as we think we're not.

And the more isolated we become, the more unhealthy, weird, damaged, ashamed, or proud we become. We may even end up becoming *all* of those—unhealthy, weird, damaged, ashamed, *and* proud. Look out! That is some kind of messed up!

GO AFTER THE ONE

As we discover the process of coming out of isolation, I want to look at an example from the Bible of a woman who encountered Jesus and reacted in a way similar to how many of us would respond (see John 4). We don't know her name, but we do know a few things about her. She's usually referred to as a Samaritan woman or "the woman at the well."

The Samaritan woman had a very painful life. Honestly, there's very little difference between where she had been and where you or

I have been—and maybe you're still just as thirsty as she was. Here's how her story begins: "So he [Jesus] left Judea and returned to Galilee. He had to go through Samaria on the way" (John 4:3–4 NLT).

This doesn't sound like a big deal, does it? However, it's a major change in direction from what was the norm at the time. Not one Jew in those days would go through Samaria if they could help it, because they thought Samaria was full of unclean, unholy people—the offspring of wayward Jews marrying Assyrians. So most Jewish people considered Samaritans

Jesus will go anywhere to meet you.

scum. They called them dogs. They would walk completely around this town, even crossing the Jordan River, just to avoid Samaritans.

At this point in the story, the disciples were not with Jesus. They had gone a different route, apparently to run an errand. But Jesus *had* to go through Samaria because he wanted to reach this woman. Jesus would have gone *anywhere* to meet her. Time and time again, he broke the rules of religiosity and every custom in his culture just to go after one person. And nothing has changed. Jesus will go anywhere to meet you.

So Jesus went to meet this Samaritan woman at a particular well in the middle of the day. Why the middle of the day? Not because it was her lunch break or a fun time to be there but because she was ashamed. Most people simply didn't go there in the scorching midday sun, and she was trying to hide out.

Seemingly out of nowhere, the woman at the well heard a voice asking, "Will you give me a drink?" (John 4:7). In the original language, this was not posed as either a question or a command. It was more like a friend talking to a friend, sort of like if you were at a friend's house and you said, "Hey, get me something to drink, bro!"

You can always tell who your friends are—when they're at your house, they don't even ask. They just open up the fridge and grab something. And when they're over, you don't care if the house is a mess, because you're with someone who knows and accepts you—just as you are.

This was how Jesus was relating to her. You may argue that he just met her. No, he knew her since she was in her mother's womb! He knew everything about her, and this is why he could be just like a friend. He is a friend—a friend of sinners. So he just said, "Give me something to drink."

She looked over at him, trying to check him out. The voice of the man didn't confuse her, because she was very accustomed to the voices of men, as we'll see in a minute. However, she was startled because when she looked at him, she immediately noticed that he was Jewish. And she knew that Jewish people hated her people.

But even in a land his people typically despised, Jesus didn't hesitate to go where he needed to go to meet someone in need. Today he still never hesitates to go around the barricades between where you are and where he is.

ARE YOU CRAZY?

Not only were the Jews against the Samaritans, but men didn't think much of women in those days. As harsh as it was, women were usually regarded more as property than as human beings. So Jesus was breaking two barriers by talking to this woman! It had to have piqued her interest. She listened, probably with a bit of skepticism. She wasn't closed off and wrapped up in herself, but she *was* reluctant. She wasn't ready to put her guard down completely, because she didn't really know who she was dealing with, but she could tell she was dealing with someone very different from the norm. So she responded, "You are a Jew, and I am a Samaritan woman. How can you ask me for a drink?" (John 4:9).

You don't really let down your guard with God until you realize that the God who loves you *really does love you*! And the love he has for you is not what you might think. It doesn't have strings attached to it. The Bible tells us, "The law was given through Moses; grace and truth came through Jesus Christ" (John 1:17).

In him there's a perfect balance of grace and truth. He speaks the truth and he demonstrates grace at the same time. In fact, though grace and truth are both listed together, I find it interesting that the Word places grace first. Notice the order! The truth is there, but it's wrapped in grace. He convicts, not condemns.

The Samaritan woman must have really been intrigued by this point. When she said, "You are a Jew, and I am a Samaritan woman. How can you ask me for a drink?" what she meant was, "Are you crazy? Are you out of your mind?" She wasn't being rude to him or trying to shut him out. She was respectful but questioning, trying to figure out what he was doing in her space and why he was willing to break cultural standards.

Jesus looked at her and said, "If you knew the gift of God and who it is that asks you for a drink, you would have asked him and he would have given you living water" (John 4:10). In other words, he was saying, "You have no idea how great a day this is. This is a really good day for you right now."

Verses 11 and 12 continue the dialogue: "'Sir,' the woman said, 'you have nothing to draw with and the well is deep. Where can you get this living water? Are you greater than our father Jacob, who gave us the well and drank from it himself, as did also his sons and his flocks and herds?'"

I am convinced that the Samaritan woman recognized immediately (as would many of us, for that matter) that she was confronted by God in person, or at least by a person of God. Later, who Jesus was became totally clear to her. She knew who she was, and she knew exactly what she was hiding, the skeletons in her closet. She was probably thinking, "If you are who you're implying you are, then what about the things I've done? What about the fact that I'm a Samaritan and I'm even shunned by my own people? If you want me to dare to step out of my isolation, which I'm not going to do, by the way, then let's have some answers to these questions!" She really doesn't want to come out of isolation, but I'll show you that in a few minutes.

Jesus was moving the conversation toward the eternal, toward the needs of her soul, which he always does with people. Jesus probably pointed over to the well as he told her, "Everyone who drinks this water will be thirsty again." But then he went on: "But whoever drinks the water I give them will never thirst. Indeed, the water I give them will become in them a spring of water welling up to eternal life" (John 4:13–14). Jesus was thinking about much more than just a drink of water in the noonday sun.

LIVING WITH FIVE MISTAKES

He was talking about water that would quench her thirst, so she let down her guard and trusted him a little. Maybe she was thinking, "Hey, this guy's not so bad. Maybe I can get some kind of miracle water out of this thing." Or maybe she was thinking, "This will solve my going to the well in 107-degree heat every day! I'll never have to feel ashamed again, because if I drink this water, I can just hole up in my house forever. I'll never have to face those people again!" So she responded, "Sir, give me this water so that I won't get thirsty and have to keep coming here to draw water" (John 4:15).

A long pause. Then he threw her a curveball by saying, "Go, call your husband and come back" (v. 16).

She probably thought, "Hmm, what's this guy up to?" Since she didn't know, she responded by telling the truth, sort of: "I have no husband" (v. 17). Not exactly the truth, but not a lie either—a good safe answer for this stranger. Maybe you've been in that kind of situation before. You may be in it right now. You feel pretty good, not because you're doing all that great but because you've learned to isolate what's really hurting inside of you from what you project on the outside. You tell people only what you have to in order to get by.

But Jesus looked at her, and with the total acceptance that only he provides, he nailed her. "You are right when you say you have no husband. The fact is, you have had five husbands, and the man you now have is not your husband" (v. 17–18).

Can you imagine? I'm sure she was thinking, "*What* is going *on?*" Her biggest fear had just been realized—she'd been outed, seen for who she really was, her soul laid bare. She was hiding the truth, and Jesus brought it up in broad daylight. Not what she was expecting. She was definitely caught off guard.

She couldn't just come out and say, "I've had five husbands." But Jesus presented it in such a way that she was able to come clean and feel his acceptance at the same time. The way he handled it is a lot gentler than the way any of us would have! He never brings up anything in your life to leave you there to die. He only brings it up so you can get free from it. Saved from it. Healed from it.

This lady had five failed marriages. Five times she went to the altar with confidence that maybe this one would work. "I do." "I do." "I do." "I do." "I do." But every time it ended with, "I don't." And now she was just living with a man because she didn't want any real commitments. There was no real love, just someone close enough to ease some of the pain.

You may be thinking, "Well, at least I'm a better person than her." No, by God's count, we all have made at least five mistakes in our lives. And many of us are living with another mistake now. The reason many of us are not engaged relationally is that we don't want anybody to know what's really going on in our lives, whether it's a bad marriage, rebellious kids, messed-up finances, or a heavy secret. Maybe if we pretend it's not that bad, it'll feel better than it really is.

I don't know about you, but I would love to be able to read somebody's heart like Jesus read the Samaritan woman's. Wouldn't it be so cool if you could know what others are thinking or everything they've done? But we can't. In order for us to come close to knowing people the way Jesus did, we have to get connected in long-term relationships. We don't get real with other people by friending them on Facebook. We get real with them over time as the relationship is solidified and proven to be safe and secure.

Remember, Jesus related to the woman at the well as her *friend*. He carefully coaxed her out of isolation. He didn't judge or condemn her. He just listened and understood and offered her a way out. And he wants us to do the same thing the Samaritan woman did that day: talk about it and share it with others. "Then, leaving her water jar, the woman went back to the town and said to the people, 'Come, see a man who told me everything I ever did. Could this be the Messiah?' They came out of the town and made their way toward him. . . . Many of the Samaritans from that town believed in him because of the woman's testimony" (John 4:28–29, 39).

RIGHT ABOUT NOW

Later, when the disciples came back from their errand, they were still their same old selves. They were selfish. They saw Jesus talking to the woman, and then the townspeople coming to see Jesus too, but they didn't ask, "What's going on?" They didn't ask, "What can we do to help?" They asked, "What's to eat?" Yep, it was all about them. They were thinking, like we so often do, "It's all about *my* life, what my schedule's about, what my weather's like, what I'm gonna do, what my kids are up to, and what's in it for me." We all have this gravitational pull to our own little world.

Jesus looked at them and said, "I have food to eat that you don't know about." But they still didn't get it! They responded, "Oh, so Jesus has already eaten, but what about us?" Jesus just looked at them and said, "My food is to do the will of the Father. I'm gonna tell you right now: I need you boys to lift up your eyes and see what's really going on around here. Do you see what's happening? I want you to lift up your eyes. And don't say later—now is the time!" (see John 4:27–38).

His message is also for us today. It's like an urgent plea, a warning. Now is the time. *Now.* Don't say later. Now is the time to come out of your hole. Come out of isolation. Get in community with others—real community, not just one-sentence status updates or wondering what's for dinner. Find out what's going on with your friends. And tell them about what you're facing, *before* you get to a place where the Lord has to track you down at high noon in the heat of your life! Be honest with somebody. You don't have to make five more big mistakes.

Scripture says that if you confess your sins to God, he'll forgive you (see 1 John 1:9). And that's beautiful. He forgives you of your sins! But hold it—it also says that if you confess your sins to *somebody else*, then you'll be *healed* (see James 5:16). Think about that! There is much more to living life than forgiveness. I'm definitely not dismissing the importance of forgiveness here. But we also don't have to live our lives knowing in our heads that we're forgiven but still feeling wounded in our hearts. We can be healed.

ROLL CALL

The Bible says that God knows everything. He knows the past, he knows the present, he knows the future. The Lord knows what you did a year ago, but what's really hard to wrap your brain around is that he knows what you're going to do five years from now! Ten years from now! Twenty! All the mistakes, all the failures, all the times you'll disobey. But he still loves you. He chooses to be around you.

I don't know about you, but if I were God and I knew everything, I wouldn't be like that—I'd be mad at you all the time for stuff you haven't even done yet! You'd get up in the morning and say, "Lord,

I love you. Lord, I've been enjoying my walk with you. Lord, I'm so in love with you."

But there I'd be. Quiet. Just looking at you.

You'd say, "Lord, what's wrong? Lord, I don't understand! Lord, I've been doing well lately!"

I'd just stare at you.

You might respond again, "Lord, what's wrong? You act like you're mad at me!"

I'd look at you and say, "I *am* mad at you."

You'd look kind of shocked and maybe say, "But I've been doing so well."

And I'd respond, "Yeah, but I'm mad at you for what you're *going to do sixty-three years from now*!" This is the way I would be if I were the all-knowing God.

Jesus, on the other hand, definitely had a more loving purpose in mind as he went out of his way to reach the Samaritan woman. And I believe that with his example, the Lord is also trying to show us what we need to be like around others. Of course, we can't be perfect like Jesus, the Son of God. *But we don't have to be.* God seems to delight in using not just regular people but especially those who've blown it! If you think about the heroes of the faith, the people in the Bible who God used in a big way, they were also people who made big mistakes, sometimes *huge* mistakes! And some of them had problems and personal issues they never overcame (this side of eternity, that is). Just consider a few from this list:

Noah was a drunk.
Abraham was an old man—way too old (100!) to have a baby.
Isaac was a daydreamer.
Jacob was a liar.
Gideon was scared all the time.
Moses had a stutter.
Rahab was a prostitute.

David was an adulterer, and he covered it up with murder!

Elijah was suicidal.

Isaiah preached naked—talk about nasty!

Ruth was a widow.

Jonah ran from God.

John the Baptist belonged on *Swamp People*—the dude ate bugs!

Peter denied even knowing Christ.

Zacchaeus had short man syndrome.

Lazarus died, for heaven's sake, and God used him!

The disciples couldn't even stay awake for an hour to pray with Christ.

Paul (when he was Saul) self-righteously persecuted Christians.

Timothy had too many ulcers.

Paul (after his name change) got shipwrecked and wound up in jail.

MESSED-UP TO MIRACULOUS

Just like God used Noah the drunk, Rahab the prostitute, and Jacob the liar, he used the Samaritan woman to reach others. He didn't want her to stay holed up in her home forever, totally accepted and loved by him but not telling others about it. He wanted her to share what he did for her, to not only receive forgiveness but also repeat the story by reaching out to others like herself.

God wants to use you too. No matter what you've done or what secrets you have. You see, our enemy has only so many tricks up his sleeve. He's really not very creative! Guys generally go for "the three g's": girls, gold, or glory. Or all three! And women? Similar—guys, gold, or glory. We all fall for the same tricks of the enemy, and then we end up believing the lie that we're the "only one" who ever did. We end up feeling dirty and ashamed, unwilling to believe God not only forgives us but also loves us and created us for a glorious purpose. We must stop believing these lies!

The result of these lies is always the same: isolation. And who wins? Nobody, because when you are isolated from friends, everybody loses, because you were made unique by God. Nobody else was made to be exactly who you are. Nobody else can follow the exact calling God has on your life. Nobody else can make the same contribution you make. You are unique! You need others, yes—but they need you too!

I believe that God can give you vision and values that can merge right into your life, right where you're at. I'm convinced that what's got us jacked up the most is that we never get past our shame to do anything for God. We think we have to be perfect before God can use us, but we're wrong about that. God loves to use messed-up people! The Samaritan woman was messed up. Yet God healed her heart, then used her to turn a whole region around.

And it's not just people in the Bible—it still happens today. I've seen countless examples. One is a man who attended our church for years without really growing

> **We think we have to be perfect before God can use us, but God loves to use messed-up people!**

or getting involved but just showing up. We tried several times to help him get some traction. He had been very successful in many ways, but spiritually? Stuck. Recently, however, he has found his purpose, and it happens to be in the one weak area of his life. He's now connecting with and helping people who are bound by the same stronghold that had him, and he's no longer stuck!

I really don't know how we would have survived (or even *if* we would have survived!) when we first planted New Life Church if we didn't have real friends we could be transparent with. In fact, the ARC, the organization I mentioned earlier in this chapter, started when a few friends who had already planted churches told us that they wanted to be there for us when we opened our doors. They supported us through prayer, sending people to our first service, sending staff if we needed help, and assisting the church financially.

Greg Surratt is the visionary behind that. It started when he guaranteed us several thousand dollars a month to help us out during our first year in ministry. When I asked him what motivated him to do this, he responded, "Because we started without anything, without any support, and it was just too hard." And so the ARC informally began when he offered that support to me and to Chris Hodges.

After just a few months, I was able to tell Greg that we didn't need any more of his money because we were making it on our own. He immediately replied, "Okay, do you know anyone else I can give it to?" I thought, "Who *are* you? Are you Jesus or something? Where does this come from?" Then we started dreaming about being able to give ideas and financial support to church planters, partnering with them to plant successful churches all around the country. And that's exactly what we've been able to do.

Today close to four hundred churches have been planted successfully in the United States through the ARC. I think it has a lot to do with pastors who are not living alone. They now have friends who give their resources, their time, and their prayer—pastors who call each other and drive to other cities to help out. I thank God that I'm a part of a movement that is continuing to grow. Ministry is tough when you're alone. Life is tough when you're alone, and we all need to have relationships.

You also can have relationships that count. No matter where you are or what you've done, you can still be used by God to make a huge impact on this world. It is not too late for you! In fact, the very point where you're struggling right now is probably the point Jesus wants you to talk to somebody about. Chances are, the person he places on your mind to call might surprise you with the truth that he or she has been facing, or has faced, a very similar thing!

When we come out of isolation and share with someone else what we're struggling with or going through, we find we are actually shedding God's light on lies we've believed about ourselves. And then we find we've made, and become, a deeper friend in the process. His truth sets us free, and we are healed. God loves using messed-up people!

4

RESCUED

How God Saves Us from Our Traps

A few years back, my wife, Michelle, and I celebrated our twentieth anniversary by going on a cruise to Jamaica. We visited a museum that focused on Jamaica's slave trading days, and I was stunned by an exhibit labeled "The Human Trap."

It honestly caught me off guard because I had never heard of such a device. Apparently, slave traders would put it down in the ground and cover it with leaves and twigs, and then when someone came along, the trap's metal jaws snapped around their ankles. To me it looked strong enough to break their ankles, but regardless, they definitely weren't going anywhere.

Examining the sharp teeth of the trap, I was struck by how often we still become ensnared, only now we're usually captured by traps of our own making. We get stuck and don't know how to get out. We want to be free. We want to be successful, to be real and honest and open, but we don't know how because of this trap we're in. And the harder we work to relentlessly pursue our own plans for our own lives, the tighter the trap gets around our legs, until we're bleeding, our bones are broken, and we believe not only will we never be able to walk again but we may just bleed to death right there. Scripture has a promise for those of us who have pursued our own plans for too long: "Many are the plans in a person's heart, but it is the LORD's purpose that prevails" (Prov. 19:21).

THROWING IN THE TOWEL

I'm convinced God loves it when we get on board with his plans. While some of his plans may always remain a mystery to us, he still has many plans he wants to reveal to his people. Ultimately, it's the purpose of God that prevails. That seems to me like another good reason to get on the same page with him and discover the freedom to be our true, best, authentic selves. I don't know about you, but I've read the end of the book, and here's a spoiler alert: we win! Still, some of us are stuck.

A few years back, I went through a very difficult time with my health. I started out losing my voice, then ended up with the flu for a long period of time, and that moved into bronchitis. But I kept going. I had a fever of 102, but I kept on speaking every weekend and pushing myself to go, go, go. I wasn't getting enough rest, and I wasn't taking care of myself. That only made me more stressed and more determined to push through regardless.

I had made such big plans for that year and couldn't bring myself to meet with my staff and admit my sickness—partly because I couldn't admit it to myself. You know you're really sick when you quit taking showers and start taking baths!

Finally, I saw a doctor who flat out told me, "You've got pneumonia," and then proceeded to tell me what I needed to do in order to be well. I had been so stubborn and refused to acknowledge what was clear to everyone around me. I had some big plans, but the Lord was showing me, "You can't do it without me. Look at you! You're stuck! You gotta have me." The Great Physician always makes house calls.

You may be in a trap right now too, and you don't really see a way out of it. Maybe it's your job and the constant fear that you're about to be laid off. It could be your finances and denial about how deep in debt you really are even as you continue spending more than you make. Or it might hit closer to home: your marriage is eroding, and day by day the two of you grow farther apart. Maybe it's your kids. Or a secret addiction. Fill in the blank with your own personal human trap.

Regardless of the specifics, I've noticed that we tend to reduce our dreams and our life's plans down to whatever size trap we're in.

We settle there. What could have been a stall-out that should have lasted for a day, a week, or a brief season turns into a breakdown that lasts a long time. And like someone mired in quicksand, the more we struggle in our own power, the deeper we sink.

To break free and stay free, you must know that God has a plan but also that the enemy has a plan. These are not my ideas. This is in the Bible, right there in John 10:10: "The thief's purpose is to steal and kill and destroy" (NLT). This verse is talking about Satan and his primary motivation. His plan is to destroy the plans God has for you. He wants to kill them; he wants to annihilate them; he wants to crush you and me. He hates us. But the rest of this verse is really cool. Jesus says, "My purpose is to give life to you in all of its fullness. I'm the Good Shepherd, and the Good Shepherd lays down his life for his sheep" (see John 10:10–11).

> **Do you think God came to earth and went all out by giving his life and then rose from the dead just so that you can barely get by in your life?**

Here's a question. Do you think God came to earth and went all out by giving his life and then rose from the dead just so that you can barely get by in your life? So you can struggle with addictions and have a marriage that feels like a trap in itself? So you can get through another week and barely make it, week in and week out?

There's *no way* that can be the plan!

Some people think that the purpose of God is that we give our lives to the Lord so that one day we get to go to heaven. That's cool, but that's not the only plan of God. Even Jesus prayed to the Father, "Your will be done, on earth as it is in heaven" (Matt. 6:10). God doesn't just want us to spend eternity with him after we die. God also wants us to be free from our traps—free to fulfill God's specific plan for us, right here and right now!

Galatians 5:1 says, "It is for freedom that Christ has set us free." If the Lord has set you free, you are free! But then it warns, "Stand firm, then, and do not let yourselves be burdened again by a yoke of slavery." In other words, "Be careful! Don't let yourself become caught again by this trap." There will be a gradual tendency for you to go back there. When I was there, I started studying the life of Gideon because I felt like I was in a trap, and the Lord showed me that Gideon was in a trap too. But let's look at the end of Gideon's life first.

He ended up being one of the greatest heroes in the history of Israel. His story looms large within the Old Testament. He ended up with an army of three hundred that decimated an army of Midianites that was many times larger. Gideon was awesome! But he didn't start out that way.

IN THE HOLE

Gideon discovered what each of us must realize: God's plan is the key to unlocking our potential. When you're caught in a trap, your potential is caught there as well. What happens if you stay there long enough? Often you start believing that you don't have any potential. You start thinking, "I don't see how the Lord can use me again. I can see how he can use *other* people, but not me. I'm in this trap. I live here. I've settled here. I'm building camp here." You resign yourself to remaining in place, stuck in a trap.

Gideon knew what this felt like. Let's look at what Gideon was doing in Judges 6: "The angel of the LORD came and sat down under the oak in Ophrah that belonged to Joash the Abiezrite, where his son Gideon was threshing wheat in a winepress to keep it from the Midianites" (v. 11).

There are a lot of terms in here that we don't use today. I haven't talked to anybody lately (or ever) who said, "Hey, Bezet, I was

79

threshing wheat today." So let's take a closer look. Back in those days, wheat would have a lot of dirt in it. To separate the dirt from the wheat, they would thresh it by throwing it up in the air, preferably on a very windy day, over and over. It was nature's way of sifting. This made the grain more valuable at the market, and it was healthier for your family to eat.

The problem was that Gideon was doing this in a winepress. If an ancient Israelite were to read this verse, they wouldn't know whether to laugh or cry! A winepress was actually a deep hole in the ground where the grapes were, well, you guessed it, pressed so that the juice could be squeezed out and made into wine. So here's Gideon in the winepress—presumably petrified, full of fear, afraid of the Midianites, and trapped. And who wouldn't be, since the Midianites were plundering villages, stealing livestock and valuables, destroying crops, killing the Israelites, and burning down the villages? The Israelites were terrified!

God's plan is the key to unlocking our potential.

So here we find Gideon, down in a hole, throwing wheat in the air where there was no wind for proper threshing. Basically, he had movement without significance. It was pointless. It was meaningless. That's what happens in a trap. You end up moving, but nothing is really happening. A treadmill of despair.

This reminds me of something I discovered while studying World War II and tactics the Nazis used on prisoners of war. One of their favorite ways to torture people was actually not physically painful at all. Each day they would have each prisoner pick up a rock that was not really that heavy, perhaps ten pounds. They would make them march a hundred yards or so—the length of a football field—and then put their rock down, go back, get another rock, carry it the same distance, get another one, and so on, all day long.

The next morning, the prisoners would then take the rocks back to where they previously were, even to the same indention on the ground, all day long. The next day, they'd start all over again. After moving rocks back and forth, back and forth, over the same distance for days into weeks on end, the prisoners began to lose their minds! They were tortured by pointless movement, an insignificant process, and tasks that didn't matter. They had movement but no meaning.

Thank the Lord that most of us have never known the horrors of slavery or concentration camps. Yet how many people seem to live their lives trapped in the same depths of despair? It might be that their career causes them to feel stuck—they hate what they do, and all other options look like dead ends. Some are still in college, and they already hate what they're majoring in and feel it's too late to change course. They regret it, but they're too afraid to change. The years go by, and soon they're in their thirties and even more afraid to do something different, too scared to take a chance and risk losing what they have, even though they hate it. They can only look forward to the day they retire—if they live that long! Can you imagine living your life with that as your only goal—doing pointless activity without anything meaningful happening?

YOU TALKIN' TO ME?

But watch this. Judges 6:12 says, "The angel of the LORD appeared to Gideon." A lot of scholars believe that this was an Old Testament appearance of Christ. I can see how they gathered that, because later on Gideon calls this angel "Lord." Even the Bible says "the LORD" was speaking to Gideon. Ultimately, I'm not sure the identity of the messenger is as important as his message.

The good news is that no matter what hole you're in, the Lord will show up in the hole with you! You may say, "I just gotta get out of here!" But you're not going to get out and stay out without him.

The Holy Spirit draws us out of our holes. And when he shows up and says, "Hey, this is the time," take my advice: go with it. Maybe that time is now. Who knows? God may intend for this book to help you get out of your hole.

Like Gideon, we sometimes can't believe God's actually talking to us. He was in this hole, wasting his life, and the Lord spoke to him and said, "Hey, mighty warrior!" (see v. 12). Poor Gideon had to be thinking, "You talkin' to me? You gotta be kidding! I'm so afraid of the Midianites that I'm hiding down in this hole! The *last* thing I am is a *warrior*."

That would be like the Lord showing up and saying, "Hey, Bezet! Mighty cat-lover!" It's just not true. Or, "Hey, Bezet, powerful vegetarian!" No, I'm not! (I do love vegetarians, though, because they leave more beef for me!)

> No matter what hole you're in, the Lord will show up in the hole with you.

But the Lord showed up for Gideon and addressed him according to what he *would become.* The Lord was saying, as Gideon hid in this hole, "If you come with me, you will be a mighty warrior. You're *not* a mighty warrior, hiding down in the hole. But we haven't teamed up so that I can empower and lead you. It's time."

Verse 13 continues the story: "'Pardon me, my lord,' Gideon replied, 'but if the LORD is with us, why has all this happened to us? Where are all his wonders that our ancestors told us about when they said, "Did not the LORD bring us up out of Egypt?" But now the LORD has abandoned us and given us into the hand of Midian.'"

Here he was, *looking at the Lord,* and he said the Lord wasn't with them. This is what happens when you're in a hole. It's like the story about the road to Emmaus (see Luke 24:13–35). The disciples were discouraged because Jesus had died, but then he rose from the dead and walked over to them while they were totally depressed. He said,

"Hey, why are y'all so discouraged?" You would have thought they would have looked over and said, "Jesus! It's you!" But they didn't. They were in a trap—a trap of severe despair. So they looked at the Lord and said, "Are you the only one who doesn't know what's going on around here?" They didn't even see him! This is what happens when you're in a trap. You can't see God even when he's right there in front of you.

I love being around people who dream big dreams. I just love it! It's hard for me, though, to be around somebody who doesn't have *any* dreams. They're not thinking about anything that *God* wants to do. Gideon's story reminds us all: God's plan is bigger than your imagination.

DREAM AGAIN

Notice how the story continues: "The LORD turned to him and said, 'Go in the strength you have and save Israel out of Midian's hand. Am I not sending you?'" (v. 14). In other words, "Dream again! I'm not bringing you out of a hole to put you in a comfortable place. I'm bringing you out of the trap so you can do something really big that will intimidate you, even flat-out scare you. But don't forget, I'm going *with* you!" It's obvious that some of us forget about what the Lord has planned and overlook his commitment to go with us. And in the deepest, darkest parts of our hole, it can be hard to remember.

A few years ago, I had to make a sudden trip to Baton Rouge to visit my pastor because his daughter-in-law died. She was twenty-five years old. She had a form of cancer that was very treatable, but she ended up with pneumonia, and it was over. I went there to try to encourage him, and I could see, to use a movie term, the eye of the tiger still burning in him. He didn't like the saga, but you could tell that he saw this as part of what God had prepared in advance for him to do. He was still on God's mission.

My friend knew that no matter how deep our hole or how painful our losses in the circumstantial traps of life, we must keep our dreams alive. Ephesians 3:20 refers to God as "him who is able to do immeasurably more than all we ask or imagine." I like this because God isn't saying, "Don't even dream. Don't even imagine stuff." He's saying, "Go ahead, *imagine* stuff, and I'm gonna *trump* it! Whatever you dream about, I'm gonna do that and *more!*"

So many of us don't dream anymore! Sometimes I think it's because we believe we're too ordinary for God to use us. But look at the big hitters in the Bible, like Noah (see Gen. 6–8). This guy had an ordinary life. He was faithful, but it was just humdrum until God showed up and said, "I want you to build a boat—a big boat—a *really* big boat. And I want you to build it right here, because the ocean waters are gonna lift it up."

No matter how deep our hole or how painful our losses in the circumstantial traps of life, we must keep our dreams alive.

Noah said, "What? You gotta be kidding me! The nearest ocean is five hundred miles from here."

God responded, "Don't worry about that. I'm gonna bring the ocean right here."

And it happened! Noah built a boat a thousand times bigger than what his family needed. Then after Noah had done what God asked him to do and the flood had come, God said, "Now I'm going to show you my covenant by giving you a beautiful rainbow to remind you of my promise."

A few chapters later, God shows up with Abram (see Gen. 12). He says, "Abram, I want you to get in the minivan and go. Take your family and get outta here."

Abram did not respond, "Uh, I don't know. Send me an email. Give me some details." God said, "Just go." And he went.

God then told Abram, "All right, I'm going to establish my covenant with you . . . with circumcision."

Abram said, "Circumcision? Can we maybe come up with a different sign? I mean, Noah got a rainbow! Can we come up with a hand signal, maybe? *Something?*"

I'm kidding about that, I hope you know, but here's the deal. One of our problems is that we remember all the stuff we *can't* do. "You can't do that. You're a Christian!" And so on.

I'll tell you a better place to live. Live around what *you can* do, what *we can* do—with God! It's much more fun than what we *cannot* do. The cannots are there, but when you see what you *can* do, the cannots are not even a hassle, because they're just a temporary nuisance. You just need to know what you *can* do *with* the Lord.

That's how dreams get started.

I was so proud of Boudreaux and Thibodeaux a while back. They had a dream of going to Hawaii. Even though it was an expensive undertaking, they never lost hope and had in fact worked for years to save enough money for the trip. They finally had enough and booked the first flight out of Baton Rouge—first time they'd ever flown too!

Well, an hour or so into the flight, they heard a loud noise: *boom!* The pilot came on the overhead speaker and announced, "Ladies and gentlemen, we just lost an engine, but the plane is perfectly able to fly with three engines. However, we're going to be about thirty minutes late." Boudreaux and Thibodeaux just looked at each other and shrugged.

A little while later, they heard another loud noise: *boom!* The pilot came on again and calmly stated, "Ladies and gentlemen, we just lost a second engine, but the plane is perfectly able to fly with two engines. However, we're going to be about an hour late." Boudreaux and Thibodeaux looked at each other again, then went back to munching on their peanuts.

A little while later, they heard another loud noise: *boom!* Again the pilot came on the speaker and stated, "Ladies and gentlemen, we just lost the third engine, but the plane is perfectly able to fly with one engine. However, we're going to be about an hour and a half late."

Boudreaux looked at Thibodeaux and said, "Man, if we lose that last engine, we gonna be up here all day long!"

GET OFF YOUR "BUT"

Let's get back to Gideon. What did he do when the angel of the Lord showed up and told him to go save Israel? Instead of getting excited or curious about the angel's greeting, Gideon responded, "But . . ." (Judg. 6:15). Now, this might offend you, but I'm convinced every time we use the word *but*, what we're really saying is, "Here are my excuses." As Christians, we all seem to want to stay on our "buts" instead of reaching up to take God's hand.

God says to us, "This is what I want to do." And how do we respond? "But I can't. But I'm the weakest in my clan. But I'm the weakest in my family. But I can't talk in front of people. But I don't know how. But, but, but . . . !" Some of us have little *buts*. Some of us have really big *buts*. But this is what we all have to get off of: our *buts*! We give excuses and God says, "Get off your *buts* and let's do something together."

So many people settle there. Young women send my wife, Michelle, emails that say, "I met this guy, and I think he could be my future husband, and he loves God, but all he wants to do is have sex with me." She tells them what I'd tell them: "Don't settle there! You don't want a fixer-upper!"

Some of you may be saying, "I'm just in college, man. I can't do anything for the Lord yet. I'm too young! I don't have the experience. I'm not smart enough." Sorry, not gonna work. The Bible says, "Don't let anyone look down on you because you are young, but set an example for the believers in speech, in conduct, in love, in faith and in purity" (1 Tim. 4:12).

Have confidence in who you are in Christ! God doesn't see the obstacle facing you; he sees the potential in you. Look through the Bible. Remember, David was anointed king as a teenager—and he killed Goliath when he was "little more than a boy" (1 Sam. 17:42). Mary? She birthed Jesus at about fourteen years of age.

You might say, "Well, my issue is not that I'm young. My issue is that I'm too *old*!" That's not gonna cut it either. Consider that God showed up to old Abraham and said, "Look, I know you're pushing a hundred years old, but I want you to go register at Babies 'R' Us, because I'm gonna hook you up."

After Abraham stopped laughing, he said, "Boy, Lord, that's a good one—I'm a hundred! And who's gonna be the mama?"

God said, "Sarah." It seemed the joke just got crazier and crazier—after all, Sarah was pushing ninety! But it happened (see Gen. 15–21).

God doesn't look at our excuses and say, "Oh, I see. I didn't realize you had *that* problem. I forgot about that one. You're right, you need to stay in the hole." Instead, God replies, "Hey, I can do *anything*. I've built interstate systems through the Red Sea for millions to cross. When I'm around people who are blind, they see. When I'm around dead people, they live again. I'm not intimidated by your excuses. Come out of the hole. Get out of the trap and let's go do something."

One day shortly before my pastor's daughter-in-law passed away, twelve hundred young people were on the front lawn of the hospital in prayer for her to live. I tried to encourage my pastor by reminding him of something he'd told me: "Faith will only take you so far. It's the grace of God and the presence of God that will take you the rest of the way."

Maybe you don't have the faith to get out of the hole, but if you'll team up with God again, you'll live again. Grace will take you there. I often tell our pastors, "Look, you can doubt your potential. I do it all the time. But don't ever doubt your call and that God is with you."

Do you ever live in doubt? That's a tough life. But God is saying to you, "Hook up with me, and let's go do this together."

WE ARE NOT OKAY

Recently, we did something in our church that we'd never done before. We publicly admitted a major mistake we'd made in our teaching. We had always said the same thing, year after year: "You can come to this church for the rest of your life and never get involved, and you'll be okay! You'll be able to grow, you'll learn the Word, but you'll never be as strong as you could be."

"You'll be okay"?

We always said that, but now we know that lives are best changed *outside* the four walls of our church in real community. Doing life together is what New Life Church was founded on. You have to be connected. You are *not* okay if you're not connected. In fact, if we continued to let our people think it's okay not to be connected, then essentially we would be saying, "It's okay if you're not telling anybody what's going on with you," which means, "It's okay if you're faking it."

You are not okay if you're not connected.

Once we realized this, the first thing we had to do was publicly admit we'd been wrong. But we went way beyond that. We based an entire months-long campaign around the theme "We Are Not Okay." That was so hard for me! Why? Because my name, Bezet, is spelled P-R-I-D-E! I'm sort of kidding about that, but I have had to learn to let the Lord work pride out of me and humility into me. I had to come clean. I had to put my agenda down. I had to make an appointment with my people and tell them, "*We are not okay.*" We had to get real about where we really were, not where we were pretending to be or hoping to be someday.

GET IT OUT

What about you? What is it the Lord is asking you to put down—*right now*? Your agenda? Your calendar? Your Facebook status updates and 140-character tweets? Maybe. Try this. Pick up your phone again, only this time use it for what it was originally intended for—to make a phone call. Go ahead. Call someone and tell him or her what trap you're in.

Don't go to the next chapter until you actually punch in seven or ten numbers and phone a friend. Find somebody you can tell everything to. Somebody who knows you and cares about you. Somebody you can be real with. And then? Be a little bit more honest. *Tell. Them. Everything.* Get it out.

But let me caution you about one thing before you speed dial and share some true confessions. Many people have good intentions of being real when they phone a friend. The problem comes when a guy who has a struggling marriage picks up his phone and calls an old *girlfriend*! That is *not* what I am talking about. The friend you need is the friend you can safely talk to—the friend who will protect your integrity. If you don't have that kind of friend, ask around for someone who is trustworthy. That kind of friend is not as hard to find as we pretend it is.

It might take some courage to overcome the whisper that says, "They'll condemn you for telling the truth." But that's the enemy talking to you! Romans 8:1 says, "There is now no condemnation for those who are in Christ Jesus." None! The Holy Spirit brings conviction to our hearts, yes. But only to make us uncomfortable enough that we want to do something about it. Remember—*he loves you too much to leave you where you are.*

Did you make the call? Yes? Good! Chances are your friend was blown away by your honesty, and his (or her) respect for you just went up about twelve notches, because *he* wasn't willing to call *you* first and tell you the truth about what's going on with him! Ha! See how this works? Don't worry. You'll be able to turn the tables soon and help your friend through some stuff too.

Maybe the thing that stopped you in the first place is that you've been hurt in the past. It may still be holding you back. At some point you may have vowed, even subconsciously, that you wouldn't let anybody hurt you again. A lot of Americans don't go to church anymore because they don't want to be hurt again. I hate that parts of the body of Christ are turning people away from exactly what they need. I hate that for many people the church isn't a safe place anymore. But we're not designed to live on an island. So even though it's a little uncomfortable right now, if you've taken that first step by making the call, you're in a really good place. And if you want to take the next step, read on.

5

REAL FORGIVENESS NEVER FORGETS

But It Always Sets Us Free

Like most of my family, my uncle Ottis and aunt Margie were real characters. One of my favorite stories about them involves a trip they took through Texas. Now, if you've ever had to drive through Texas heading west—*all* the way through Texas—then you know how bored they must've been! It's like that movie *Groundhog Day*, with the same cows mile after mile after mile! The *same* cows! I don't know how anyone ever drives across that state.

Ottis and Margie were driving with their son through the central plains of the Lone Star State when she announced she had to go to the bathroom. She began complaining about needing to stop—and believe me, she could gripe *loud*! Since they were in the middle of nowhere, Ottis, usually a pretty laid-back guy, said, "There's a gas station where you can go to the bathroom in about sixty-five miles."

"Are you kidding me?" she said, and she continued griping about how badly she needed to go. Finally, they saw the exit and he pulled in to the gas station. Aunt Margie ran in, then immediately ran out and hopped back in the car. "It's nasty in there! I'm not going here!"

Uncle Ottis said, "Whatever!" and they took off again. She still had to go, of course, and resumed complaining. After a few miles and a lot more nonstop griping, he talked her into going on the side of the road. Despite her protests, by this time she knew she had no choice. He pulled over and explained how she could open the rear door of the car to give her a little privacy in case someone drove by. She got out, a couple minutes went by, and then he heard the door shut. Assuming she'd gotten in the backseat with their son, who'd been sleeping, Uncle Ottis drove away. However, their son had woken up and closed the door—Aunt Margie was still on the side of the road going to the bathroom! To make matters worse, the next exit was over sixty miles away. She had to wait nearly two hours for him to turn around and come back to get her. Now Aunt Margie really had something to gripe about—for the rest of her life!

HURTING PEOPLE HURT PEOPLE

This incident was one of many that became legendary in our family. But despite Aunt Margie's griping and Uncle Ottis's oversights, it was clear they loved each other and remained committed to their marriage. And the secret to their relationship was clear: forgiveness.

There's more here than just a lesson in making your marriage last. Maybe coming out of the trap of being fake and embracing what God has for the real you also rely on this fundamental part of the Christian life. A big part of getting out of the trap—for good—is recognizing that you may have some forgiving to do.

At the end of the last chapter, I asked you to make a very important phone call to a friend to make a kind of confession, if you will, as a step toward revealing the real you to someone else. Think about what you talked about with your friend. Does the story you told them have any loose ends? Is there anyone you still feel bad about? Are you angry or hurt because of what somebody else did to you? Maybe ashamed because of what *you* did? Sometimes when we start talking to our friends about what's going on, it almost feels like the problem is getting worse, not better. That's probably true, because there's some undoing, even some healing, that might need to happen.

Sometimes the people who love us the most are the people who hurt us the most. They offend us over and over again. I believe God knows that the closer we get to one another, the more likely we are to hurt one another, because we all have problems and weaknesses. So he commands us to forgive one another. I'm convinced the Lord says this so clearly because he knows what happens to a soul when there's no room for forgiveness. You get trapped, bound up by unforgiveness, and that grows into what the Bible calls the root of bitterness.

> **God wants us to experience freedom, not the chains of anxiety and roots of bitterness that bind us when we don't forgive.**

But God wants us to be honest and open with one another, to be real with one another, and to practice forgiveness. He wants us to experience freedom, not the chains of anxiety and roots of bitterness that bind us when we don't forgive. The Bible says, "So if the Son sets you free, you will be free indeed" (John 8:36). Notice what this is actually saying: *If* means it's not automatic; we have to let him. "The Son sets you free" means *he* does it, not us. And "you will be free indeed" means totally and completely free!

God sets us free because he knows otherwise we will become ensnared in our sins and infected with bitterness from wounds inflicted by others. He sets us free so that we can fully experience the authentic life for which he created us. He can't stand to see his people in chains, trapped without room for his Spirit to work.

WHAT IT'S NOT

One of the major barriers to this freedom is our inability to forgive and to ask for forgiveness. I once heard Joyce Meyer say, "I have found that no other ingredient damages the heart more than the issue of unforgiveness." I would add that no other ingredient prevents us from being real more than the issue of unforgiveness.

We all struggle with this area. Why? Because everybody has issues. I have issues, and so do you. Listen, if you don't think you have an issue . . . then that's your issue right there! From time to time, all of us, including me and including you, don't forgive people well enough. I'm convinced most of us don't even know what forgiveness really looks like. In fact, maybe it would help us to understand it and practice it more if we considered what forgiveness is not.

First, true forgiveness is not something you have to wait for someone to ask you for. Sometimes we think we don't need to forgive until somebody *asks* us to forgive them. But you really can't find anything in the Bible that'll back up this approach.

Similarly, forgiveness is not a conditional contract. Real forgiveness is unconditional. Nothing is attached to it. It's not a contract. It's not real if you say or think, "I will forgive you *if* you never do it again" or "*if* you do this first." No. That is nothing more than a negotiation, a trade.

When Jesus stretched out his arms on the cross, he said, "Father, forgive them, for they do not know what they are doing" (Luke 23:34). He didn't say, "Father, forgive them *if* . . ." None of us *deserves* to be forgiven by Christ, but aren't you glad he extended his forgiveness toward you?

The great Roman historian Cicero said that people who were being crucified at the time of Christ were in such agony and pain that they would hurl blasphemous words, cursing everybody there. So it was very common for the captors to cut out the tongue of the person being crucified. We know they did not do that to Jesus, because on the cross, up until the moment he died, he was making seven last statements. He was forgiving everyone around him (see Luke 23:34). He was forgiving the thief on the cross (see Luke 23:43). He was making sure that his mom was taken care of (see John 19:26–27). He was talking to the Father, aiming his hard questions at God, wondering aloud why it felt like God had forsaken him (see Matt. 27:46). He acknowledged his humanity by saying, "I am thirsty" (John 19:28).

And then he declared, "It is finished" (John 19:30) and "Father, into your hands I commit my spirit" (Luke 23:46).

In the midst of his suffering, Jesus continued to exemplify the importance of forgiveness even when your life is not going so well. Why did he forgive? So we can. Why is it important? Because he knows what happens to the soul of a man or woman when they live with bitterness.

Real forgiveness is also not retaliation. Look at Joseph in the Old Testament (see Gen. 37–50). He was sold into slavery by his own brothers. They lied about him. Then Potiphar's wife told everybody that he tried to rape her, when really she was the one trying to molest him. But when he ran away from her, she lied and he ended up in prison. (As far as we know, she thinks she got away with it. But what she doesn't know is that this story is included in the most popular book ever written!) Joseph could have become a very bitter person, but he didn't. And he never tried to retaliate against any of those who hurt him.

Real forgiveness does not minimize the seriousness of the offense.

On the other hand, real forgiveness does not minimize the seriousness of the offense. You may have a tendency to think, "Okay, I'll forgive. I guess it didn't hurt me that bad." No, it *did* hurt you. "Well, I guess it wasn't a big deal." No, it was a *really* big deal. "Well, I guess they didn't mean it." Maybe they didn't mean it; maybe they did. None of that diminishes what happened.

When Joseph saw his brothers years after they sold him into slavery, he had full authority to kill them, but instead this is what he said: "You intended to harm me, but God intended it for good to accomplish what is now being done, the saving of many lives" (Gen. 50:20). He didn't pretend that he wasn't devastated by the betrayal of his brothers, let alone the other things that happened to him. Immediately after saying these words, he left the room, broke down, and wept. But because Joseph had not allowed bitterness to take root, he was able to forgive.

FORGIVE AND REMEMBER

Sometimes we think that forgiveness means you have to forget. The motto is "You have to forgive and forget." Show me a Bible verse on that! No, you forgive, but you still remember. You don't even have the capability of forgiving and forgetting. In fact, the more you try to forget, the more you remember, because you're mentally rehearsing the event! So let yourself off the hook. Don't try to force yourself to forget an offense prematurely. When you forgive, you release the memory from having a grip on you.

When Joseph finally faced his brothers again, after many years, he remembered what they had done. He didn't forget. He even reminded them, "You intended to harm me" (Gen. 50:20). It had been many years since they had betrayed him and sold him into slavery, but he forgave them. He was even able to bless them, provide for them, and be reassuring and kind in the process (see Gen. 50:21–22). You know it's real forgiveness when you no longer want revenge. When Jesus does a great work in you, having to retaliate for the past isn't necessary anymore.

Finally, when somebody hurts you, you may think, "Well, if I forgive them, then I have to trust them. I have to let them back in." For example, maybe you're a woman whose husband abused you. I've been in these homes. Abuse is real. If you're being abused, then to you I say, "Run for cover." I'm also not saying you can never trust again, because certainly people make comebacks. I see it often. But I'm not talking about trust. You can forgive them and maybe trust them later, or maybe not. But forgiveness applies either way. Trust has to be rebuilt; trust has to be earned. Forgiveness is built on grace and is unconditional. You don't do it because they deserve it. You do it because it's what God has done for you.

WHEN THE PRESSURE IS ON

People who have been forgiven are people who forgive! I know a lot of people say, "Yeah, God has forgiven me, but I've done one or two things that no one could ever forgive me for." These people have trouble forgiving others because they don't feel like they've been completely forgiven. Look at this Scripture: "Make allowance for each other's faults, and forgive anyone who offends you. Remember, the Lord forgave you, so you must forgive others" (Col. 3:13 NLT). When we experience the fullness of God's grace, we are creating room and finding the space to forgive others who have hurt us. The reason some of you haven't forgiven others is that you haven't really received it!

If I took an orange and put it under pressure, trying to squeeze it with the strength of my big, strong arm, I could make it explode and fly at least a hundred feet. Okay, not really. But when an orange is squeezed, what will fly out of it? Orange juice! Why? Because when pressure is applied, what's on the inside will be what comes out. If you have unforgiveness on the inside, during times of pressure, that's what will come out. And remember, fresh-squeezed bitterness never tastes good!

I'm convinced that the number one problem in the body of Christ is condemnation—of both ourselves and others. Consider what Jesus said about how to pray: "Forgive us our debts, as we also have forgiven our debtors" (Matt. 6:12). Basically, he's telling us, "The way I want you to pray is like this: 'Okay, God! I need forgiveness in my life. I want to be clean. I want to be like you! So the way I want you to forgive me is with equal measure to the way I forgive other people.'" God says, "Not only do I want you to *live* that way, but I also want you to *pray* that way."

If you struggle with this concept, you are not alone. Peter traveled with Jesus as one of the disciples for three years and still didn't understand this! So he went back to the Lord and tried to turn forgiveness into a math problem. "'Lord, how many times shall I forgive my brother or sister who sins against me? Up to seven times?' Jesus answered, 'I tell you, not seven times, but seventy-seven [or seventy times seven] times'" (Matt. 18:21–22). The number seven is special in Scripture. Peter knew that. He knew God created the world in six days and rested on the seventh, then called that day holy. He'd read story after story in Scripture that talked about seven days of this, or seven weeks of that, or seven years until something happened. It was everywhere! Peter (and every other Jew who was paying attention) understood that the number seven represents wholeness, completeness.

Maybe Peter was trying to impress the Lord by acknowledging that he understood it took more than just a customary, "You're forgiven." When Peter said, "Hey, how about seven times?" he was probably thinking, "Jewish law says just three times, so I'll double it, add one, and get a perfect answer." But maybe he was also thinking, "But do I have to forgive him completely?"

Jesus said, "No, not seven times, but seventy *times* seven." In other words, not just completely but completely *and* continually. Jesus was basically saying, "Every day, for the rest of your life, choose to never live around unforgiveness again. Always be a person who wants to forgive, and when you need to forgive, do it completely and continually." But Peter still didn't get it, so Jesus jumped into this parable:

> Therefore, the kingdom of heaven is like a king who wanted to settle accounts with his servants. As he began the settlement, a man who owed him ten thousand bags of gold was brought to him. Since he was not able to pay, the master ordered that he and his wife and his children and all that he had be sold to repay the debt.
>
> At this the servant fell on his knees before him. "Be patient with me," he begged, "and I will pay back everything." The servant's master took pity on him, canceled the debt and let him go.
>
> But when that servant went out, he found one of his fellow servants who owed him a hundred silver coins. He grabbed him and began to choke him. "Pay back what you owe me!" he demanded.

His fellow servant fell to his knees and begged him, "Be patient with me, and I will pay it back."

But he refused. Instead, he went off and had the man thrown into prison until he could pay the debt. When the other servants saw what had happened, they were outraged and went and told their master everything that had happened.

Then the master called the servant in. "You wicked servant," he said, "I canceled all that debt of yours because you begged me to. Shouldn't you have had mercy on your fellow servant just as I had on you?" In anger his master handed him over to the jailers to be tortured, until he should pay back all he owed.

This is how my heavenly Father will treat each of you unless you forgive your brother or sister from your heart. (Matt. 18:23–35)

God wasn't fooling around on the subject of forgiveness. It wasn't a suggestion. He demanded that you forgive, because forgiveness releases you but unforgiveness controls you. It affects every aspect of your life and ultimately your destiny.

TEN THOUSAND BAGS OF GOLD

We all have accounts we have to settle. In this parable, ten thousand bags of gold—or talents, as such an amount of money was called—was an astronomical figure. One talent back then equaled about fifteen years' worth of wages. So it would take him 150,000 years to pay off this debt! Some say it could have been as much as $6 billion. This person owed *a lot* of money.

Since this passage of Scripture is all about our debt to God, we're reminded that there's no way we could ever repay the debt we owe. Our loving Father, however, extends his grace to us for a debt larger than we can ever imagine. Aren't you glad he was willing to forgive you? It would take 150 lifetimes to even think about all we owe him!

A lot of us say, "That's my debt, so I'm gonna try to pay it myself. I'll give to charity and treat people nicer than I have to." No matter who you are, even if people tell you every day that you're a super good person, you could never pay your debt of mercy to God! If you went to Burger King and said, "I want two Double Whoppers with extra mayo and bacon, extra large fries with ketchup, and two apple pies with ice cream on top," and then added, "and a Diet Coke, please," you have to realize something. That Diet Coke does not make up for all the calories and fat-laden items in your order! One Diet Coke can't cancel out all the bad stuff. Similarly, no matter how hard we try, we can never earn God's forgiveness by what we do, say, or try to be. He gives it to us freely. We only have to accept it.

Back in Jesus's day, there were no bailouts, no bankruptcies. You had to pay your debt, and if you couldn't pay it, they could throw you in prison. And if they wanted to, they could have your children and your wife thrown into prison or sold into slavery. This detail in the parable reminds us that sometimes your unforgiveness hurts your whole family. Your sin hurts me, and my sin hurts you. If I go out and live any way I want, would it hurt my wife? My kids? You bet!

When the indebted servant fell on his knees and begged for his master's mercy, he promised something he couldn't deliver. No matter how hard he tried, there was no way he was ever going to pay back that enormous amount. What happened? The master had mercy on him. And that's exactly what happened to all of us—our Lord had pity on us! This Scripture is clear. God didn't look down at us like Donald Trump evaluating a potential employee on *The Apprentice* and think, "Well, you know what? I like their spunk! They have potential. They might be worth hiring and investing some time in." No, absolutely not!

You must know that when God looks at you and me, he sees us as we are. He looked at Rick Bezet, saw me without him, and had pity on me. He didn't have to do it, but it's his nature. He loves his children no matter how unlovable we may feel, seem, or actually be.

When God looks at us, he sees us with compassion, not condemnation. When Jesus looked at people, he always loved what he saw.

We're told that when Christ saw the crowds, he had compassion on them (see Matt. 9:36). When Jesus saw the leper in Mark 1, his compassion moved him to heal the man (v. 41). In Luke 7, his compassion for the widow who had just lost her only son moved him to bring her son back to life. The shortest verse in the Bible is "Jesus wept" (John 11:35). He had compassion on those who were having a difficult time. He has compassion on you. God is the God of compassion—he loves to love you! It's simply who he is.

> **When God looks at you and me, he sees us as we are.**

WANT SOME MORE, BIG BOY?

This truth can be hard for us to grasp. I confess, I am not always the best at forgiving. Sometimes I even keep score. I remember one time coming home and hearing about how a boy had hurt my daughter at school that day. She was only about eight at the time, and as I was hearing about how this boy had pushed my daughter and embarrassed her in the foyer of the school, I was flat-out *mad*! My wife, Michelle, was acting so mature and spiritual, saying, "We just need to forgive. We need to pray!"

Are you kidding me? I was thinking, "I'm gonna teach my little girl how to go back and kick that boy. How to kick him in a certain place. A certain place that will cause him to double over, and when he doubles over, she can knee him in the nose, and while blood's coming out, she can say, 'Want some more, big boy?'" That's what I was thinking! As you can tell, I still have to work on this forgiveness thing a little bit. I am so thankful that Jesus had compassion on me.

Unfortunately, not everyone is willing to accept what God offers us. You see, two things might happen when you realize your debt. One, you might fall on your knees. That's a good idea! Or two, you might go into slavery—bad idea! Remember, Galatians 5:1 tells us it was for freedom that Christ set us free. The very next verse warns us to be careful not to go back into slavery. Watch out! Unforgiveness grabs you. Unforgiveness says, "You owe me!" Unforgiveness takes matters into its own hands.

Now here's where the parable gets really interesting. Remember that guy who fell on his knees and begged, "Please forgive me of my huge debt"? His master replied, "Okay, you're forgiven." This same guy said, "Thank you so much!" and walked out without truly realizing what he had just been given.

Like so many people who go to church, hear about God's grace and forgiveness, smile and nod, and then walk out unchanged, this guy had not experienced the gift of forgiveness. It's almost ridiculous to consider, but look what happened. This very guy who had just been forgiven as much as $6 billion walked out, grabbed this other fellow who owed him roughly $17 (100 denarii), and began to choke him. Say *what*?

When we step back and consider how anyone could be so unaware, it's hard to believe. The scene almost doesn't make sense, but the Lord uses this story to draw our attention to what's happening in our own lives. How could a guy who's just been forgiven billions of dollars turn around and be angry over such a small thing?

This guy is crazy—but, when I think about it, I've done the same thing! I've been angry over minor things and almost gotten caught in the act. For example, I remember having a heavy sense of God's grace and love for me one particular Sunday. That same week, I got ticked at somebody on the freeway. He was whipping up behind me, then driving beside me, then cutting in front of me and slowing down. Finally, it seemed like he was trying to run me off the road. I was so mad I actually wanted to hurt the guy—then I noticed it was someone from church! What would have happened if I had made the wrong gesture at him? I was instantly seized with conviction, because I knew if it had been a stranger, I might have given in to that temptation, or at least held on to my anger in my heart. The point I'm trying to make is that we all have a tendency to be angry over little things when we've been forgiven much.

Notice that at the end of the parable the master calls this guy "wicked" for not being able to forgive someone else's small debt after he's had the debt of a third-world country forgiven (Matt. 18:32). He is ticked! He's angry that this guy doesn't get it. That's because God knows there's no way we can experience the reality of his mercy and forgiveness toward us and not extend it to others. His forgiveness is humbling. It strips away the layers of our pride and our pretending.

There's no way we can experience the reality of his mercy and forgiveness toward us and not extend it to others.

Grace is like paint stripper that removes all those layers and layers we've wrapped ourselves in. God gets us down to the natural wood of who we are, not the laminate veneer that we tend to show others. He makes us real. "He forgave all our sins. He canceled the record that contained the charges against us and took it away by nailing it to the cross" (Col. 2:13–14 NLT).

BITTER OR BETTER

When you decide to forgive somebody, you start growing. When you make room for forgiveness, God's presence invades that space. But when you don't, you're stuck—you lock yourself in place, and it's not a safe place either! In fact, the Lord even pointed out in this parable that the servant would be turned over to the jailers to be tortured until the debt was repaid (see Matt. 18:34).

So often this process takes place without us even realizing how imprisoned we've become. Have you ever met somebody who started drinking a little bit in their teens, then got addicted to alcohol, then started doing some drugs, then became a meth head? Okay, fast-forward ten years. You haven't seen that person since they were fifteen, and now they're twenty-five. Guess what? They'll act just like they did when they were fifteen because their life has been on hold. Their maturity level will be the same as it was before.

This is exactly what happens when somebody doesn't forgive. It's like being stuck in the past. Bitterness does this. Bitterness is like drinking poison and waiting for the other person to die. It tortures *you*, not the other person. We think we're giving it back to the other person, but we're only hurting ourselves. On the other hand, forgiveness releases you from that torture. When you decide to forgive somebody, you start growing.

> **Bitterness is like drinking poison and waiting for the other person to die.**

I can almost guarantee that if you don't practice forgiving others, you will never fully become who you were created to be. You will never become the real you without forgiving others. You can never move forward into the future God has for you if you're stuck in the past. Recently, a woman told one of our pastors, "I feel like if I stop hating the people who hurt me, they'll start winning!" My response: "No, *you'll* start winning!"

Jesus made it clear not just in this parable but through his actions, his teachings, and his death that forgiveness—or a lack of it—determines how you will grow spiritually. He said, "For if you forgive other people when they sin against you, your heavenly Father will also forgive you. But if you do not forgive others their sins, your heavenly Father will not forgive your sins" (Matt. 6:14–15).

You might not realize it, but there are people out there who need to hear this because of you. You've hurt some people. So have I. I determined a thousand times when I was in Bible school that I was going to be a pastor who loved people and believed in them. But then this lady who was a lawyer and her daughter started manipulating the church. I could not wait to meet with her and set her straight. She came into my office, and I started asking questions. She was a master debater. She started building her case like she was in front of a jury.

All of a sudden I got so mad that I started verbally blasting this lady. She came back at me, and it was like a war in my office. I kicked into anger and bitterness that I never knew I had. I went after her, and she started backing down, and I went after her more, and she backed down more, and I started feeling good about my cocky self. I went after her more, I got loud, and she retreated even farther. I finally said, "Now, see? You don't have *anything*. Now *get outta here*." She stood up, I walked her to the door, and I watched her walk down the hallway. She looked about ten years older than when she had come in.

Then it hit me: I had become the very person I never wanted to be. It took me a long time to track that lady down and get in touch with her. I was able to forgive her, and I was able to forgive myself. But she never came back to church again, and it saddens me to this day.

PRACTICE IMPERFECT

Most of the time I tend to be a joyful person, but sometimes no matter how hard I try, I realize I'm still human. An incident comes to mind in which I learned another humbling lesson about forgiveness. A pastor friend of mine fell into sin, then he covered it up and lied, and then he was busted on CNN.

Everyone was thinking, "What in the world's going on with him?" I retreated and hibernated in my office. I remember looking at the wall and thinking, "I'm gonna punch my hand through the sheet-rock!" (I clearly could have done it—I've already explained the massive strength I have, right?) I was in shock and my emotions ran the gamut—anger, sadness, frustration, disappointment, betrayal, and more anger.

My wife was worried about me. My friend Billy Hornsby called me on the phone and said, "Bezet, you're gonna ruin your life if you live this way. You need to forgive him." I got on my knees, repented of unforgiveness, chose to forgive my friend, and immediately felt set free.

I don't want to go back there. I don't want to live there. I want to live in the freedom that God promises to you and me. How do we remain free and walk around being fruitful and confident and enjoying an authentic relationship with God and others? I'm convinced it has a lot to do with forgiving people and not keeping score.

No matter how difficult it seems, you must forgive if you want to be real. In your marriage, forgive your spouse. Otherwise, you'll get competitive and start keeping score: "Who's contributing the most around here? Who's raising the kids the best? Who's working the hardest? Who's bringing the money home? Who appreciates all that I do? Who's meeting my needs?" And on and on and on. Is this really where you want to live? Do you really want to be that person who knows God's forgiveness one moment and then tries to choke someone who owes you the next?

When you decide to forgive somebody, you're saying, "You don't owe me anymore, and I'll never try to collect from you. This is the way I choose to live." This is fundamental to being real. Fakers pretend to forgive and then choke everyone around them. People who are transparent and real practice forgiveness on a daily basis.

Let's practice right now. Say it. Right where you are, think about someone who's been preoccupying your thoughts because of how they hurt you. Think of them and say, "I forgive you. I release you. You don't owe me anymore. I break the power of unforgiveness and bitterness in my life through the power of Christ and the power he has given me to forgive!"

The next time it happens—the next time somebody hurts you, or a car cuts you off on the freeway, or someone says something mean or unkind about you—let it go. Forgive again. Release. Receive more of God's forgiveness for you! It will change your life. It's the key to being real.

6

CROWDS, COMPANIONS, AND CONFIDANTS

Being Real as You Relate

everal years ago I performed a wedding that had all the features of a fairy tale—beautiful dress, great food, the works. However, all the time, money, and energy invested in making this ceremony an over-the-top celebration still couldn't produce the happy ending the bride so desperately wanted. Oh, the groom showed up—it wasn't that. But not many other people were there.

All her life the bride had dreamed about having a really big wedding. So as soon as her boyfriend popped the question, she booked the church chapel far in advance of the ceremony. But when I say "chapel," I'm not talking about a quaint, little room with six pews—this chapel was huge! It held hundreds and rivaled the main church sanctuary for square footage.

As soon as I heard what she was planning and where it would be held, I immediately sensed a problem. I had known this young lady for years while she was involved in our youth ministry, and I knew she didn't have many close friends. In fact, she didn't have many friends at all. Why? Mainly because she was mean—mean as a snake! She treated people like they were inferior to her and often publicly criticized those around her. She would gossip behind the backs of her "friends," and eventually people caught on and stopped hanging around with her. They withdrew because of her demeanor.

During the rehearsal the night before, this bride fussed at people here, barked orders to others there, bossed her fiancé around, and just generally made being obnoxious an art form. Now, I understand that brides are under a lot of stress, especially right before their big day, but unfortunately this was not unusual behavior for this woman.

No one told me how many invitations had been sent out, but based on the catering alone, I suspected it must have been two or three hundred. However, as we got close to the time for the ceremony to start, I noticed the chapel was still almost empty. We waited a few minutes longer before we started, but no one else showed up. If not for her family and the groom's friends, the room would have been entirely empty. It was very sad, and even though she was mean to the core, I felt sorry for her.

How did this girl not know that this could happen? How did she miss the fact that these people she considered "friends" did not see her the same way? Didn't she have anyone around her who could tell her the truth?

No one wants an empty church when they get married. We want special people to celebrate our amazing moments with us. The good times and the bad. We want friends around us, the real kind, the ones who know us and love us anyway. We want people who care about us to be there when we need them.

BLIND AUDITION

Earlier in this book I told you that one of our worship leaders came in first place on the TV show *American Idol*. Up until the time Kris became a contestant, I didn't watch it much. I was amazed to see how many people would turn out to audition when the *Idol* bus cruised into their area and the judges began screening would-be superstars.

As I watched the early weeks of the show, I was even more amazed that so many of the contestants were really bad. I mean terrible! When they sang, I wanted to close my ears or throw something at the TV. As they warbled and screeched out some song I couldn't even recognize, I'd think, "What's wrong with you? Don't you have any friends who can be honest with you and tell you that your voice is awful?" Apparently not.

On another singing competition TV show, *The Voice*, they have "blind auditions," which makes sense to me. The judges don't see the contestants; they only listen to them to decide if they should go forward. But nobody has deaf auditions! If you like to sing, you need to have someone who will tell you the truth about how you sound. I love to sing—in the shower, with the car radio, in church—but I don't think I'm going to cut an album anytime soon. Although I will say, I probably sing better than some of those people I saw on TV!

How about you—do you have the kind of friends who can tell you the truth about your audition on *American Idol*? Have you ever had this kind of really good friend? The kind who could tell you anything and it would be okay? Someone you knew would be loyal to you for your entire life?

Many people travel through life without a friend like this. They live in a lonely place made up of plastic friendships and imaginary closeness, only to find out later that what they thought was a friendship was really a mirage in the desert. Some people experience this painful realization at times when they want to celebrate, like the young bride I told you about. Other people discover their lack of true friends when they hit rock bottom and need someone to help them through an unexpected crisis.

We're designed to need friends and to be a friend to others.

If we are going to be real, both with ourselves and with God, we also must be real with those around us. God made us to be part of a community, to belong. We're designed to need friends and to be a friend to others. Too often, though, we get caught up in trying to please would-be friends for the wrong reasons. We compromise who we really are in an attempt to be who others want us to be.

Other times we become so insecure and afraid of rejection that we only show others our mean, manipulative side. We think that if we remind people how inferior they are, they'll feel like they need our superiority. But most of us know that neither of these masks ultimately works. We develop real friends only when we're willing to be vulnerable.

The good news is that it's not too late. No matter how old or young you are, good friendships are possible. It doesn't matter how many mistakes you have made or how many people have hurt you. God created you to have close relationships, but you may require some reprogramming in your life to accept that blessing. Are you ready to change? Are you ready to put down the masks and become the kind of friend you'd like to have? Then keep reading—it's time to get real with your relationships.

ENGAGE THE CROWD

Good relationships happen on many levels, from the most intimate friend to the multitudes of people you encounter as you live your everyday life. Each of these levels is important and can contribute to your well-being in different ways if you allow them. While our individual relationships are unique, I'm convinced most fall into three categories: crowd, companion, or confidant.

I've drawn this conclusion not just from my own experiences but from what we observe in the life of Jesus. Could we ask for a better role model? Jesus was a friend to *everybody*! Nonetheless, he doesn't necessarily expect you to be friends with all seven-plus billion people in the world because he knows you're not God. If you don't know that yet, you might need to be reading a different book! I'm kidding, but my point is that Jesus had lots and lots of friends.

Everywhere he went, he healed people, drove out demons, fed people, taught those who wanted to listen, healed more people, and stood up to the religious accusers. Every time he did something amazing. Once his public ministry was launched, Jesus didn't need social media; his every interaction with people was so powerful and real that they were instantly changed, and the news spread like wildfire!

As more and more people began following him—literally—a crowd formed. And even as the crowds grew larger and larger, he was okay with it. He loved the crowds because he loves people. He had enemies too, but he had a lot more friends. In fact, we know that at one point at least five thousand people followed him around a lake (see John 6:1–2)! That's a lot of people! It was often impossible for him to get away from them, as there were so many who were simply drawn to him. I call this kind of relationship "the crowd."

CROWD CONTROL

It's important to notice the crowd, because if you're not noticing, if you're wrapped up in your own world, doing your own thing, you might not realize that our world is rapidly changing! You might miss out on both giving and receiving a blessing. Let me give you an example.

A while back at the Arkansas Dream Center in downtown Little Rock, one of the volunteers took time away from her job to help make a young girl's life a little better. They were just going to hang out and have some fun together—lunch, a movie, and shopping at the mall.

The girl had recently had a birthday. At the mall they were trying on jewelry when the girl said, "You know what I really wanted for my birthday? I wanted one of those necklaces with a big *T* on it. You know, like the ones for church and God." She had no idea, no reference point, for understanding the meaning of the cross, or even what to call it! To her, it was a letter of the alphabet.

Where was this again? In Arkansas! The Bible Belt! It's important to pay attention to what's going on around you. If you don't, you will become increasingly irrelevant in a culture that is increasingly hostile to anything that has to do with God. You will miss out on obvious opportunities to share your faith in the most natural of ways. You never know when a conversation with a child, or a kind word to a stranger, or a simple act of courtesy might change someone's life—even your own.

God wants you to have a broad network of friends just like he does. You've got to have friends in the crowd, friends you can play a game of pickup ball with, or go shopping with, or watch the Super Bowl with, or whatever you're into. Some friends are close and some are closer, and most you probably won't know beyond a certain surface level. That's okay! If you don't have friends in the crowd at various levels of closeness, you end up being deep all the time because you have few acquaintances, or you end up being superficial because you don't have any close friends.

Being deep isn't a bad thing, but it also isn't necessarily healthy to do all the time. You start taking yourself too seriously. Then you don't experience joy. Then you stop having fun. Then no one really wants to be around you. Then you feel hurt and rejected and vow not to need anyone ever again. And then you don't have even the friends you had!

The opposite, of course, is true about having only acquaintances—you don't ever take yourself seriously, you don't check yourself, there's no accountability, and it's pretty easy to figure out where you'll end up after that. You know lots of people and mingle in lots of different crowds. But you don't know anyone beyond those crowd-level relationships. You keep everything based on appearances and polite small talk.

KNOW YOUR CROWD

No, interacting with the crowd in your life needs to strike a balance. Not everyone from your crowd will become your companion or confidant, but some might. Over time the people in your crowd will change as your life changes. When you move to a different place, take a new job, or change churches, your crowd will change.

As your kids grow up and you're involved in school and extra-curricular activities, your crowd will evolve as well. One year you know all the parents with kids on your daughter's soccer team. The next year it might be all the parents with kids in the drama program. We may not be able to control our crowd, but we can change with it.

So what does it look like to have a healthy relational base? You have to know your crowd. The crowd gives you perspective, and the more diverse your crowd, the better perspective you have—on the world, on life, on your own situation. These are people you run into every day—at the grocery store, the ball field, church, or wherever. Without trying to be their best friend, you should have some awareness of everyone you interact with on any given day. It's important to be connected to the large-scale community of people. I'm not just talking about the church or your local church—I'm talking about e-v-e-r-y-b-o-d-y!

> **The more diverse your crowd, the better perspective you have.**

How do you find that healthy balance with your own crowd? Or maybe you feel like you don't really have a crowd in your life right now. In either case, finding the right relational balance is pretty easy. In fact, it's actually quite simple once you get used to it. It can be summed up in three words: *start noticing people.*

It doesn't matter where you are or what you're doing. Just notice the people around you! Notice if Carol the grocery cashier is in a good mood or not. She usually is, but was she today? Was the teenager waiting on you at the restaurant doing a really good job? In addition to leaving a big tip, maybe you should tell her how much you appreciated the great job she did. What about your mechanic or the dentist's receptionist or the co-worker assigned to work with you on a special project?

You don't have to be everybody's closest friend, but do notice them and acknowledge them. One person is not really better than anybody else. We tend to get stuck in certain roles and certain scripts that prevent us from being real with each other. That cashier is more than just the person taking your money and giving change. She's a mom, a sister, a wife, a daughter, a cancer survivor, a best friend, and a volunteer for her church. The guy who's trying to help you fix your computer is also a single dad, a military veteran, a deacon in his church, and a gourmet grill master.

We're all human, no matter what we're doing! We just have to remember this and look for those opportunities to bring God's love into the lives of everyone we encounter. Jesus didn't meet, heal, and hug everyone in every crowd, but he had a huge impact on each individual nonetheless. We can do the same.

TRAVELING COMPANIONS

It's also important to be able to look at a crowd of people and pick out several people you know. Those are your friends, the people you would hang out with in a much smaller group than your crowd. These are the friends I call companions. It's a really good thing to have a close group of friends with whom you travel down life's roads. These are your buddies, your girlfriends (if you're a lady!), the band of folks you enjoy hanging with. Your traveling companions.

Boudreaux and Thibodeaux are like that—best buddies. They love hanging out together. In fact, they're always trying to bum food off each other. Once Boudreaux was carrying a bag, and Thibodeaux asked him what was in it. "Boudin sausage," he answered.

Thibodeaux said, "I bet I can guess how many are in 'dat bag."

Boudreaux answered, "I bet you can't, but if you can, I will give you both of 'em."

Thibodeaux replied, "I bet dere's three!" Now that's a real friend—somebody who will reach over and just eat whatever's in your bag.

When Jesus first started his ministry, he was practically unknown. Yes, he had made some headway a few times before—the priests at the temple probably remembered him from when he was twelve years old. Not a whole lot is written about his life up until the time he started his ministry, so we can only conjecture about how many people actually knew about him. But after John the Baptist baptized him, one of the first things he did was choose some friends to hang out with—Peter, Andrew, James, and John.

> As Jesus walked beside the Sea of Galilee, he saw Simon and his brother Andrew casting a net into the lake, for they were fishermen. "Come, follow me," Jesus said, "and I will send you out to fish for people." At once they left their nets and followed him.
>
> When he had gone a little farther, he saw James son of Zebedee and his brother John in a boat, preparing their nets. Without delay he called them, and they left their father Zebedee in the boat with the hired men and followed him. (Mark 1:16–20)

When Jesus chose these men, they didn't really know what he knew all along—that he was choosing them for a much deeper relationship. They thought maybe they were just men in the crowd, but by the end, they had become his closest companions.

I love the fact that Jesus was real. The early church was real too. The book of Acts says, "Every day they continued to meet together in the temple courts. They broke bread in their homes and ate together with glad and sincere hearts" (2:46). They were real! This is what God wants. A lot of people want access to the power that was available to the early church, but before you get that you have to be authentic. This is so simple but so vitally important.

THAT'S WHAT FRIENDS ARE FOR

Notice something else we see in Acts 2:46: they ate together. *Together*. They were friends! Real. Friends. What a concept!

If you want to have good friends, start with finding people you want to hang out with. You may not get to choose the crowd you belong to, but you do choose your friends. You need the crowd, and you choose your friends. Your companions are your friends—the set of people you'd want to go on vacation with and even bring their families. You know that you can hang out with them and be yourself. They're like-minded, or at least close to being like-minded. You have some common ground with them, whether it's golf or bridge or scrapbooking or whatever. Get plugged into a group of people who do something you like to do.

From there, how do you develop your friendships? If you want to have good friends, it's a really good idea if you learn to *be* a good friend. Spend focused time with your chosen friends! Let them speak into your life, and speak into theirs. Say happy birthday. Write thank-you notes. Send a text of encouragement for no reason. Show appreciation. Be someone that others appreciate. Be a real friend. Be transparent.

Also, it helps a little bit to be approachable. If you're not approachable, if people just don't want to be around you, ask yourself why. Are you angry or short-tempered? Anger is usually a mask for pain. Almost always, if you find an angry person, what you've really found is someone who has been wounded but hasn't faced his or her pain. This, of course, goes back to what we talked about in our last chapter on forgiveness. While reflecting on why you might not be approachable, check to see if there's a reason why anger is still there. You really need to release that to God if you're carrying it, because it's only hurting you. Be real when you've been hurt—forgive! Be willing to be vulnerable sometimes.

Or maybe you're not approachable because of something else. You could have gotten into the habit of being a complainer. Maybe you've met that couple before—"David and Debbie Downer"! I'm pretty sure they're not just in Arkansas! You think you deserve something you didn't get or haven't gotten yet. Maybe it's a promotion or a raise, or maybe something like the respect of your own spouse. Who knows? But one thing I do know is that sometimes we get so wrapped up in what we want or what we need that our focus gets more and more on ourselves rather than on others' needs. We become more and more selfish, because all we think about is what we need, which is what *selfish* means.

Do you know what the cure for that is? You might be surprised! Once again, it's very simple: "Give, and it will be given to you. A good measure, pressed down, shaken together and running over, will be poured into your lap. For with the measure you use, it will be measured to you" (Luke 6:38). If you read this verse, and it seems counterintuitive (that's a fancy way of saying "backwards thinking"), then you're right—it is!

If you want to have more friends, then you should spend time *being a better friend*. Then when you're a better friend to others, it will return to you, but not in the same measure! Whatever you give returns to you "running over."

Whatever it is you want to receive, give that away.

This could go both ways. If all I give out all day long is complaining, then I will soon find that I have a good measure, pressed down, shaken together, and running over—of complaints! I definitely don't want that. I hate complaining. But I *love* encouragement! And so, the more I encourage, the more I am encouraged! *Whatever it is you want to receive, give that away.* Pour it out on everybody you know, and see what happens. Get to where you don't think about yourself all the time, because that will definitely destroy you.

If you're still struggling to make real friends, jump in at your local church and serve somewhere. Volunteer as a greeter or in children's ministry or picking up trash. Everybody needs help, and when you work side by side with other people toward a common goal, guess what? You get to know them. You make friends. You become companions.

CONFIDANTS

Remember the phone call I asked you to make earlier in the book, at the end of chapter 4? You probably called your best friend or maybe a couple of close friends. If they weren't your best friends then, they are definitely a lot closer to you now than they were last month! These are your confidants.

A confidant is a person you call when big things happen in your life—a big win or an embarrassing loss. If you were to fail at something, this is the person you would call first. If you won the lottery, this is the one friend you'd tell (maybe the *only* person you'd tell,

Without a confidant, the deepest part of a person is alone.

depending on your family!). When you're at the end of your rope and don't know how to handle your kids or your marriage or your job, this is the friend you want to share it with. A confidant is loyal and knows how to keep a secret.

It takes time to become a confidant and patience to find one if you do not currently have a person like this in your life. But without a confidant, the deepest part of a person is alone. My brother, Randy, is a confidant to me. My friend and fellow pastor Chris Hodges is a confidant to me.

I remember one time when one of my sons had a problem. Well, he really had two problems. The first problem was that he played Xbox way too much. It was like he was addicted to playing video games. So Michelle and I told him he had to limit the amount of time he played. We would monitor how much time he was on it and tell him when time was up.

But we'd find him playing when he wasn't supposed to be, so we cut it out altogether. Only then we'd find the game controllers in places where they weren't supposed to be! Obviously he was sneaking around playing games behind our backs. I was beside myself about how to handle this, so I called one of my confidants for some wisdom on how to handle it. He didn't necessarily have the answers, but it helped just to have another father provide me with some perspective on how to deal with my son.

Confidants are a select few people who will tell you the truth (hopefully in the nicest way!) when you ask them, "How am I doing? Is there anything I can do better?" You want to be a little more careful here—don't choose a confidant who posts everything anyone ever tells them on Facebook. That's not a confidant. That's a problem! Confidants are carefully selected people. They're trustworthy.

Not every relationship is the same. Jesus had a "twelve" (the disciples), a "three" (Peter, James, and John), and a "one" (John). Jesus was around the crowd a lot of the time, but he also chose his friends, and he had a few closer friends. You'll usually find your closest companions, your "three," among your companions; and you'll find your most trusted confidant, your "one," among your closest companions.

Everyone needs to have at least one confidant. You also need to be willing to *be* a confidant. You need it, and they need it! It requires being willing to think about somebody else and listen to somebody else—really listen.

This reminds me of a time when Boudreaux was having trouble in his marriage. It just seemed to him that no matter how hard he tried, his wife wouldn't listen to him. He started thinking that maybe there was a problem with her hearing. He was very discouraged about it, so he went to the doctor and said, "Hey, man, I'm really worried about Sista Boudreaux. She not doing good at all."

The doctor said, "What's wrong?"

Boudreaux said, "She can't hear nuttin'. I talk to her all da time, but she don't hear nuttin'."

The doctor said, "Why don't you bring her in, and I'll test her?"

Boudreaux said, "Well, she ain't comin' up in here, noooo way."

The doctor said, "Well, here's a test you can do at home. Get about ten feet behind her while she's doing the dishes or cooking, and just ask her a common question in a normal voice. If she doesn't respond, take a step closer and repeat the question. If she still doesn't respond, take another step until she finally gets it, and measure how far away you are. Then come back and tell me, and I'll help her."

Boudreaux said, "Dat's a good idea. I'ma go do dat right now."

So Boudreaux went home, and when his wife was cooking dinner, he got ten feet behind her and said, "Hey, Sista Boudreaux, what's fo dinnuh?" She didn't answer. He got discouraged. So he got nine feet from her and said, "Hey, Sista Boudreaux, what's fo dinnuh?" She didn't say anything. Eight feet. Seven feet. Nothing. Six feet. Five feet. Four feet. Still nothing. He was getting more discouraged. Three feet. Two feet. One foot. "Hey, Sista Boudreaux, what's fo dinnuh?"

She turned around and yelled, "I've done told you *nine times*, we havin' crawfish pie!"

That dude was deaf, not her!

You might be pointing at other people, frustrated that they aren't listening to you, but the problem might be you! It might be me. I think we are as close to others as we really want to be. (I also think we are as close to God as we really want to be.)

GIVE AND TAKE

You actually can measure whether your friends are mostly crowd, companions, or confidants by looking at your schedule. If you want to get better in any of these three areas, change your calendar! If you're always in the crowd and you're not spending time with companions, join a small group at your church. If you're always having coffee with your best friend, join a softball team. You get the idea. To balance all three areas, it takes a little give and take.

You know you have a balanced life of healthy relationships when you have valued relationships in every area—crowd, companion, and confidant. If you're still not sure, ask your spouse and the friends you do have. They'll tell you the truth.

And I'll tell you this: everyone needs a friend to help them. Friends are the reason why we have small groups at New Life. I want friends who will help me, pray with me, believe with me, and do life with me. It's why I love small groups at our church—it's a place where you can go and grow.

You have a balanced life of healthy relationships when you have valued relationships in every area.

You need a friend who doesn't just give you what you want just to try to make you feel good. You need a friend who gives you the Word of God. In fact, Peter once responded to a crippled man who was asking for a handout, "I don't have a nickel to my name, but what I do have, I give you: In the name of Jesus Christ of Nazareth, walk!" And then it says that Peter "grabbed him by the right hand and pulled him up. In an instant his feet and ankles became firm. He jumped to his feet and walked" (Acts 3:6–8 Message).

I need friends like that. I need to be a friend like that. And so do you. I don't know if you have good friends right now. But I do know that if you're in a relationship with somebody that's strong and healthy, it's because you've invested in it. It's not happening by accident. You have to put in some time, and it can be tough. It's difficult to build real, transparent friendships. It takes enduring effort—there's no doubt. But remember this: when you invest in real relationships, the dividends are always worth it!

1

INTELLIGENT DESIGN

He Made You on Purpose

When I was younger, through mutual friends at church I met a guy named "Big Mike." If you saw him, you would know why they called him that—he was big, and his name was Mike! This dude weighed three hundred pounds, and he was solid muscle on a six-five frame. He was clearly very strong but seemed very humble about it. It was almost like he didn't even realize his own strength.

One day a group of us went to an arcade, and there was a game where, when you punched this bag, you earned a strength score from 0 to 1,000. I got up there, put my money in, and said, "Watch this, Big Mike! I'm going to show you what life is all about!" Then I swung and hit that thing, and it got to 300 or 400 points—just a little bit lower than my SAT score. Then I looked at Big Mike and said, "Come on! I want to see what you can do!" But he didn't want to. We wandered the arcade and played a lot of games, but he wouldn't do it.

On the way out, right before we had to leave, I talked Big Mike into it. I put up the money, and something came over him. He zoned in with a purpose, like he was going to knock all the air out of that bag. He reared back and hit it square, right in the middle. The machine powered down! I'm not kidding you—it totally powered down. He knocked that machine out! Big Mike just stood there looking at his hands.

Big Mike resisted my suggestion in the beginning, but when he finally tried it, his own strength amazed him. I believe he walked a little taller when we left that place, and he was already fairly tall.

So often we don't recognize our own abilities. We end up struggling to be authentic because we haven't learned to embrace what

God has given us. I'm convinced a lot of what we call "self-doubt" and "lack of self-confidence" is really just an inability to understand or embrace the way God made us.

FOLLOW THE LEADER

Often our problem is not that we don't have any idea about who God made us to be. Our real problem is that we fight God's design for us. It's not a question of "What does God want for me?" but rather "What do I do with what God wants for me?" It's a battle of our wills.

Even Jesus struggled with accepting what his Father gave him to do. When he was in the Garden of Gethsemane, battling with his Father to the point of sweating blood, Jesus prayed, "Father, if you are willing, take this cup from me; yet not my will, but yours be done" (Luke 22:42). He was willing, as hard as it was, to submit his preferences to his Father's. This proves how tough this battle really is. If it was a battle for Jesus, do you think it might be a battle for us?

> **Our real problem is that we fight God's design for us.**

Many people say, "God, here are my plans. Bless them." Instead of praying, "Not my will but your will be done," we're actually saying, "*My* will, *not* your will, be done." We also think that if we keep repeating our desires louder and louder, eventually God will give in. Or we go and try to find other people to confirm and reinforce what we want for ourselves. I promise you that if you want to do something and seek out enough advice, you will find people who will agree with you. But it doesn't mean that God does!

Consider Moses. He is described in the Old Testament this way: "Since then, no prophet has risen in Israel like Moses, whom the LORD knew face to face" (Deut. 34:10). He was also honored this way: "Now Moses was a very humble man, more humble than anyone else on the face of the earth" (Num. 12:3).

But Moses didn't get there overnight. If we look at his entire life, we can see a huge turning point in how he received the favor of God. He clearly made sure that not only was God in the equation, but God was *taking the lead*. In Exodus 33, God kept giving Moses bits and pieces of his purpose and plan for Israel, and Moses kept going back with objections like, "Okay, you've told me to lead Israel. Now tell me who is going with me."

God responded, "My Presence will go with you" (v. 14).

Moses went back to him again, almost arguing with God: "If your Presence does not go with us, do not send us up from here" (v. 15). That's bold! Moses basically said to God, "No way am I going *anywhere* if you're not leading!" That's how adamant Moses was about staying in God's design for his life.

As a result, God provided a clear sign to guide Moses and the people of Israel on their journey to the Promised Land. "The cloud of the LORD was over the tabernacle by day, and fire was in the cloud by night, in the sight of all the Israelites during all their travels" (Exod. 40:38). Because Moses demanded that the Lord God *lead* them on their journey, an entire nation was blessed with God's presence continually.

YOU ARE NOT ALONE

Even after we're committed to following God, we still have so many questions. Some of the questions about his design for who we are start when we're young and get more intense as we get older: "Do I play football or baseball? Should I be in the band or the choir?" Then it's "Should I go to college or take a job out of high school?" If you choose college, then it's "What college should I go to?" and "What should I major in?" After college it's "Should I get a master's degree or a job?" Eventually, you look for a job, and then it's "What job do I take? Where do I live? Which church do I go to? Who am I going to marry?"

Some questions have pain attached to them: "Lord, is my marriage ever going to work again?" "Is this blended family ever going to blend?" "Is my health ever going to return?" "Will I always be this lonely?"

Sometimes you get so desperate to hear from God that you work yourself into a state of panic instead of just trusting in him and waiting patiently. When I was single, I asked God, "Lord, is there just one person for me? What if I blow it? What if the one person you have designed for me is in the room with me, and you had to work hard to get her in a room with me, and there she is, and I chicken out and don't talk to her? Did I ruin my life, and now she's going to go marry someone else? Does that mean that I've messed up the whole system?" Sometimes the questions get out of control.

But among our many questions, there's one we must always remember the answer to: *Does* God have a plan for your life? Yes, of course he does! The psalmist wrote, "All the days ordained for me were written in your book before one of them came to be" (Ps. 139:16). Is it possible for you to actually know who he designed you to be or what his plans are for you? I believe so, but we are often not in a good place to hear from him.

I know Boudreaux is often not in a good place, but one time he dragged Thibodeaux into the mess. Boudreaux and Thibodeaux were hunting, and they killed a huge buck. They grabbed this deer by the tail and back legs and were dragging it through the woods, but the antlers kept catching the ground. (Boudreaux and Thibodeaux were Cajuns like me. I always tell people we're not the smartest people in the world—it takes us two hours to watch *60 Minutes*!) Here they were, dragging the deer by the tail, and they couldn't get the buck out of the woods because the antlers were grabbing every vine. The game warden walked by and said, "Hey, what are y'all doing?"

Boudreaux said, "We got a big buck here, man!"

The warden said, "Yeah, but you're dragging it out wrong. If you drag it by the antlers, it's a lot easier to get out of here."

He walked away, and they looked at each other and agreed that it made a lot of sense. So they went around to the other end and started dragging the buck by the antlers. Boudreaux looked at Thibodeaux and said, "Man, this is a lot easier!"

Thibodeaux said, "Yeah, but we're getting farther and farther away from the truck!"

Maybe you have figured out how to carry your life, how to grind through, but you're getting farther and farther away from the truck—away from where God wants you to be. We get distracted and worn down by circumstances, by our own selfish choices, and by listening to the wrong people.

I can't tell you about God's specific design for you, but what I can do is help you get to a place where you can best hear from the Lord. It begins when we remain humble and teachable. With this in mind, here are a handful of truths I've learned about how we can become truly real by focusing on what God wants for us.

CUT OUT COMPETING VOICES

Often we can't hear or see God's design clearly because there are too many voices competing for our attention. It's not because he's not speaking. It's that we can't hear because of the voices all around us. These other voices may be hobbies, finances, our kids, our marriage, our job, or just plain old boredom. The voice of God is not loud. In fact, God's plans are often revealed in a still, small voice, not even as loud as a whisper.

Sometimes in order to hear God, it's a matter of timing. Years ago I was able to speak at Louisiana State University's chapel the day before a game. I walked out on the field before anyone was on it. No one was in the stadium. It had room enough for 95,000 to sit there, but it was just me. I was looking around, waiting for my chaplain friend Ken to meet me. Two guys came out on the opposite side of the stadium and were talking about whether the grass on the field was ready for the game. I was far away from them but could hear everything they were saying. I wondered if it was due to the acoustics there. The next day, the stadium was packed with 95,000 people, screaming loudly. My friend tried to tell me something during an intense part of the game, and I couldn't hear it. Why? Too many voices.

So how do you eliminate distract-ing voices? One suggestion I have that works for me is to consistently open

The voice of God is not loud.

up God's Word in the morning. If you want wisdom, read Proverbs. For more of a heart after God, read the book of Psalms. If you don't know how to study the Word, meet with someone who does. Get involved with a small group that teaches the Word of God.

If you don't buy into fasting from food, at least fast from media every now and then. Turn off the computer and TV and take a break from reading blogs, magazines, and newspapers. Get alone with God somewhere for a couple of days. One directional idea from him can totally destroy what the devil has built for years in your life. We can't hear God's voice when we allow distractions. We *can* hear his voice, but only if we're tuned in.

ADMIT WE DON'T KNOW BEST

I'm a logical person, and I like to strategize. However, I've discovered—as I'm sure you have as well—that many decisions cannot be made based on logic alone. "Should I put my parents in a nursing home, or should I let them move in with me?" "Should I tell my wife what I did, or should I hold off?" "Do I start this business now, or do I wait a year?" "Do I go into ministry and give all this up?" "God? Are you there? Are you listening to me?"

God's Word tells us, "As the heavens are higher than the earth, so are my ways higher than your ways and my thoughts than your thoughts" (Isa. 55:9). We may not like it, especially if we like to rely on logic, but God is not always logical. Our minds are limited no matter how smart we may be. God knows the best solution for us before we can even come up with the right question!

Now, I'm not telling you not to use your brain. There's a lot in the Word about having the mind of Christ and being wise. But if you only go with pure logic all the time, you have to reduce God down to the size of your brain. The Bible talks about signs and wonders. Do you know what wonders are? When God does something and you wonder how in the world he did it! Logically, it just doesn't make sense to you.

When God started talking to me about moving to Arkansas, I responded, "I can't do it. I just can't go there. I don't know how to get there. I have to feed my kids. It seems like a stupid idea." Logically, what is impossible for Rick Bezet is impossible. But Jesus said, "What is impossible with man is possible with God" (Luke 18:27). When you need to move a mountain, if you just look at it logically, your logic says, "You got me on this one." But when you connect to the plans of God, you can see your mountain, but you can also see through it. You won't just talk to God about the mountain in your way; you'll start talking to your mountain about your God. There's a lot more victory in that.

Often we simply haven't brought God into the equation. Before you call a friend, your mama, advisers, and counselors, God says, "Call me! I want to be in on the design of your life." James 1:5 says, "If any of you lacks wisdom, you should ask God, who gives generously to all without finding fault." We don't ask, because we think he's just going to point out all the stuff that's wrong with us. But it says "without finding fault." He'll give generously, and even if it doesn't make sense to us, it *will* be given!

BE CONTENT WITH GOD'S DESIGN FOR YOU

I've almost quit. I'm not a quitter generally, but on the big decisions in my life, I've almost quit. I had three years left in Bible school, but it felt like twenty-five years! I had friends in Orlando who were doing quite well in business, and they were calling me to join them. "Bezet, we want to keep you involved. If you will come back to Florida, we will put you back in as a partner, and you will be a millionaire soon."

Well, sure enough, now they're all very wealthy. One of them is now worth well over $50 million. I knew they were going to do well. Although I had already seen the plans God had for me, I wanted to quit to go after something that looked better. I was tempted to not be content with who God designed me to be.

Comparing yourself to other people will hinder your ability to do the work God planned specifically for you to do. Not all people have the same assignment. For example, you normally eat a meal with a fork, a knife, and a spoon. What would happen if you tried to eat soup with a knife or cut steak with a spoon? The truth is, we need each utensil for its specific purpose!

Comparing yourself to other people will hinder your ability to do the work God planned specifically for you to do.

Now picture two different people serving the church. Person one loves to make sure the chairs are lined up perfectly. He is task-oriented, and it bugs him if things are not just right. Person two could care less about the chairs and only cares about the people in the chairs. This could create conflict, but the truth is that we need both types. The Bible says, "There are different kinds of spiritual gifts, but the same Spirit distributes them. There are different kinds of service, but the same Lord. There are different kinds of working, but in all of them and in everyone it is the same God at work. Now to each one the manifestation of the Spirit is given for the common good" (1 Cor. 12:4–7).

PUT CHARACTER BEFORE COMFORT

These principles of relying on God in order to experience true contentment can be easier to talk about (or write about!) than to practice. And for me, it all boils down to this. There is something I don't like much about God. I don't like the fact that God is working on my *character* more than he's working on my *comfort*. Too often, I have seen the Lord allow pain in my life to get me to change.

Maybe it's because he knows that the pain I would have experienced if I had stayed on my own path would have been even worse. Do you know what I mean? Sometimes the Lord will even take you out of a strong relationship just to get you to a place where you have to call on him, because it's keeping you from what he knows is *best* for you.

If you're in a battle of wills with God, you're going to hate his plans. Psalm 37:4 says, "Take delight in the LORD, and he will give you the desires of your heart." This word *delight* is similar to how a bride prepares for a wedding. Brides start working on it when they're five years old. Men don't have weddings—we get married. But *women* have *weddings*—they go for it!

Verses like this one mean that he'll actually plant desire in you. How is that? I am convinced that if you are in love with God, when you delight yourself in him, you get to do what you want to do. You *want* to do it because he plants the *desire* for it in your heart. Before you may have said, "I will never do that! I will never be that way," but suddenly you want to do it! Spend time in his presence, and his desires become your desires. You want what he wants.

DO YOU SEE WHAT I SEE?

Learning to see and hear God and then to follow him does require practice. It's a lot like learning to see something right in front of you that doesn't immediately reveal itself. This reminds me of an experience I had when seeing really was believing.

Years ago I walked into a mall in Texas and noticed a lot of people standing around staring at pictures that had a lot of graphics that didn't make sense. As I walked past, a lady grabbed me and said, "Look at this picture!" Then a guy said excitedly, "You gotta stare at it, and if you stare at it, the Empire State Building will come out right in front of it!"

I looked at it, and the lady was coaching me, "You have to let your eyes get real lazy." So I let my eyes get real lazy. Then she came back with, "You have to cross your eyes a little bit." So I crossed my eyes a little bit. I finally said, "I don't see anything!" She tried one more time with, "Well, you gotta look through the picture." I said, "I can't do that!" I left and bought what I went there for in the first place.

On the way out, I saw the pictures again, and I stopped one more time, knowing I wasn't going to see anything. I stood in front of them with a bad attitude, mumbling, "This is a bunch of nonsense. This is a joke." As I was standing there with a bad attitude, all of a sudden, the Empire State Building came out! So what did I do? I started grabbing people! "Hey, come check this out!" They would say, "Well, I don't see anything." And I would say, "You gotta stand here with a bad attitude. You gotta get a real bad attitude, you gotta be mad about it, and then you'll see it."

What was that all about? I saw something that I wanted other people to see. That's how I feel about this chapter! I desperately want you to get this—to understand with clarity that God has a real purpose behind the person he made you to be. His plans are huge, and they involve you.

FOUR THINGS GOD DOES NOT HAVE

What exactly is it that God could possibly need from us? We've spent a lot of time talking about what we need from God. We've been asking, "Who have you designed me to be, God? What are your plans for me, God?" But let's turn this around a little bit. What about God? What does God need from us? There are four things God does not have unless you give them to him:

Your *appreciation*. Getting with God and saying, "Thank you!" makes him really, really happy! He likes it. A lot! It's okay to get together with him and be thankful. He provides everything for us—our life, our breath, our food, our families, our homes, and our jobs. He likes it when we stop and notice all that he does for us every day.

Your *attention*. "Don't become so well-adjusted to your culture that you fit into it without even thinking. Instead, fix your attention on God" (Rom. 12:2 Message). Notice what this verse reminds us to do: put God first! Like any relationship, our relationship with God requires us to focus on him, spend time with him, and enjoy his presence.

Your *affection*. Hosea 6:6 says, "For I desire mercy, not sacrifice, and acknowledgment of God rather than burnt offerings." God is basically saying to us, "I don't want your sacrifice without your love. I don't want your offerings without you knowing me." God wants us to be connected with him and other people, and we can get this done when we focus our affection on him. When we love and serve others, we're showing our affection toward God.

Your *abilities*. You have had abilities since you were a kid. Maybe you were able to sell really well. Your friends had a lemonade stand. They went bankrupt. You had a lemonade stand. You made lots of money. Parents were studying what you were doing! Some of you have administrative ability. When you were growing up, your desk was always spotless and your room was always clean. Now your closet is color coordinated by seasons! It's your gift. Whatever your gift is, God wants you to use it, because that's how he made you!

You may be asking, "What is my gift? I'm still not clear about God's plan for me." Or you may be asking, "How can I use my gift to serve others when I'm not sure what my gift is?" If you don't know what your gift is, how God has made you different from everybody else, and how that fits into his plan for you and for his kingdom, there are a lot of resources out there that can help you work through discovering your personality, passions, and God-given desires, including the DISC test or Myers-Briggs Type Indicator. Find somebody to coach you through one of these resources and to help you figure out who you are and home in on what God's plan for you might be. Each time the picture gets clearer to you, celebrate it. Thank God for how he made you!

AGAINST ALL ODDS

All this takes faith. God is not going to reveal everything about his plans to you immediately. In my experience, all you can do is say, "Okay, that looks really cool," and then go for it. When we take that first step, God takes the next.

Sometimes—maybe even most of the time—the first step feels like a really big step. Sometimes it has significant risk attached to it. Take the story of Esther, for instance. In Esther 1:13, King Xerxes, who was furious with his first wife for publicly disrespecting him, chose to "consult experts in matter of law and justice," and spoke with "the wise men who understood the times," before deciding how to respond to his wife, Queen Vashti. When he had received their advice, which was consistent with the laws and culture of that time, he wrote an irrevocable edict that she would be forever banished from his court and her position as queen would be given to somebody else.

Then we read about Esther, a beautiful young woman raised by her uncle Mordecai because her parents had died when she was young. She was entered in the first beauty pageant recorded in history, as far as we know, and she won, of course. She was on her way to becoming the next queen.

Meanwhile, King Xerxes's right-hand man, Haman, was getting ticked off at Esther's uncle for not bowing down to him, so he manipulated the king into issuing another irrevocable edict, this time to kill all the Jews. (Haman got mad at one guy and decided to wipe out an entire race. It's probably safe to say that Haman had a lot of pride in him!) Next we see a snapshot of the entire nation of Israel fasting, weeping, and mourning. Fair enough—I would be too if I knew that my entire family was about to be executed! So Mordecai sent a messenger to Esther to "instruct her to go into the king's presence to beg for mercy and plead with him for her people" (Esther 4:8).

Well, Esther already knew, based on what had happened with the previous queen, that Xerxes was all about following the law to the letter. And one of the laws back then was, "You don't go to the king. Ever. If the king wants to see you, he summons you. Not the other way around, or you'll die." She was faced with a real decision: either go to the king and risk instant death, or wait it out and hope for the best. The only problem was that if she waited it out, it might possibly turn out okay for *her*, but it certainly was not going to be good for every other Jew in the kingdom. So she sent a message back to Mordecai saying, "I will go" (Esther 4:16).

Those three words, "I will go," represent bold decisiveness—what it took for her to step out in faith, not knowing what was going to happen, not knowing the end of the story, not even knowing if she was going to make it out alive. It took faith for Esther to boldly decide to get off the fence and take the risk to do what God was calling her to do. I love what Mordecai had said to her just before in verse 14: "And who knows but that you have come to your royal position for such a time as this?"

We see God's people taking a step of faith time and time again throughout the stories of the Bible: Noah, Moses, Abraham, Joseph, Gideon, Ruth, and so many more. Even in the life of Jesus, it's clear that he had to come to terms with what his Father called him to do. Even when you can't see what's coming or it looks scary and impossible, take that first step of faith, trusting that God will use it, and you, for his purposes.

Once we accept how God made us and what he calls us to accomplish through his power, we find it's pretty easy to be real. We can be genuinely excited about life because we don't have to pretend to be anything but who we are. Once I realized that God really had a good idea for me—that God's design for me was not to move to Florida and become a millionaire—I entered into a lifetime of contentment!

When you embrace *who* God made you to be and what his plans are for you, when you are able to open your hand to him and say, "Not my will but your will be done," you'll discover a whole new level of peace and contentment.

8

FIREFIGHTERS

How to Work Through Conflicts

For some reason I've always been fascinated with fire, even as a little kid. I used to love to gather sticks together and make a fire. My mom didn't like it, but I would do it anyway, and then I would add leaves and then bugs. But don't worry—I never considered adding anything else, I promise you!

While it goes without saying that even the smallest fire can suddenly become a blazing inferno, I was an adult before this really hit home. We were living in Louisiana and had just built a home in a cul-de-sac. It was moving day with lots to be done. After a bunch of boxes and trash had accumulated, I put the pile in a corner of the backyard on top of some fresh sod. Safe enough, right? I lit this on fire, and when it was going strong, I went inside the house to unpack a little more.

When I went back outside a few minutes later, my yard was on fire! And it was moving directly toward my house. I didn't have a hose hooked up yet, so I started taking water by the handfuls and throwing it on the fire. That didn't work very well, so I started stomping on it. Then the bottom of my blue jeans caught on fire!

Now, just for the record, I'm living proof that the whole "stop, drop, and roll" business is bunk. I tried it, and my blue jeans started blazing even more. So I did what anybody would do—I took them off! There I was, new to the neighborhood, and the first thing my neighbors learned about me was not my name or occupation or how many kids I had. No, they learned I'm a briefs guy. I finally managed to stomp out the fire—in my underwear. I wasn't surprised to see my new neighbors staring at me, and I think I heard one of them tell his kids never to come to our home. Not my best day.

WHERE THERE'S SMOKE . . .

I like a fireplace in the wintertime. I like the ambiance. It sets a mood and provides warmth. I like fire, but I don't like what a fire can do when it's out of control. An uncontrolled fire can consume acres of forest and wildlife, homes, businesses, even entire cities.

Unresolved conflict in our relationships is like a raging fire. Everybody knows that having a little fire is inevitable, maybe even a good thing to keep the relationship warm. But when ignored and left alone, conflicts can simmer and smolder and turn into a raging inferno that destroys the entire relationship and others around it. When the heat is turned up on our relationships, most of us let our pride, fear, and anger keep us from being honest, vulnerable, and forgiving. Unresolved conflict keeps a lot of people from being real.

Unresolved conflict in our relationships is like a raging fire.

Sometimes you can't avoid conflict, but when God is involved in it, good results can happen. I love it when God moves into a situation, controls the fire (maybe even puts it out), and changes it to a situation where he's able to move like never before. But here's the problem: a counterfeit will try to worm its way into our lives.

A counterfeit is the alternative option to God's plan that would by default bring conflict and consequence because it takes you down a different path than where God wants you to go. Counterfeit choices bring conflicts that aren't necessarily fires that you *have* to go through. Some conflicts we can't avoid, but many we bring upon ourselves because we are deceived.

For example, when Jonah received instructions from God to go to Nineveh, the Bible says he "ran away from the LORD and headed for Tarshish" (Jonah 1:3). From God's perspective (and yours, hopefully),

Jonah was directly disobeying a command of God. But from Jonah's perspective, maybe he thought his actions were justified!

We're not absolutely certain of Jonah's motives, but it makes sense to think, based on Jonah's later actions, that he simply didn't want the Ninevites to have an opportunity to repent. To Jonah, it made more sense for God to judge the city of Nineveh and be done with them. So Jonah was deceived into thinking it was okay to disobey God and go do something else. The consequence was that he then had to deal with a very unpleasant circumstance—living inside a stinky fish for three days. Would you say, "Gotta get me some of that?" I don't think so!

God gives us a warning in 1 Timothy 4:1: "The Spirit clearly says that in later times some will abandon the faith and follow deceiving spirits." This verse shows that you can be deceived, following ungodly spirits, and not even know it. Most of the worst conflicts I've ever seen have been related to deception. People don't know what it is, they don't know how to get out of it, and then when conflict happens, they just run away. They quit.

A fire inspector told me recently that there are three big problems when it comes to fire, and they relate to our relationships as well.

Smolder

A smolder is a slow-burning fire that happens in unseen places. This kind of fire can be extremely dangerous because a lot of times we don't realize what's happening until it's too late. Have you ever walked through a home and smelled an odd electrical smell? You immediately think something's not right. You ask yourself, "What is that?" You want to figure it out. You don't want to leave until you know.

Sometimes you can tell that something's not right in a relationship. Something's smoldering. Maybe your spouse is telling you that they love you, but something's not right. Their actions don't back up their words. Maybe your kids have smiles on their faces and are even saying they're doing well in school, but something's not right. Maybe your business partner is saying the company's finances couldn't be more solid, but something's not right. There's a smoldering fire waiting to turn into an inferno.

Soot

Soot can release a poisonous gas when certain items burn, especially synthetic materials. When people are trapped inside a burning building, it's often toxic soot that takes their breath away and endangers them. Their healthy oxygen gets replaced by nasty air that can kill them unless they get out.

Similarly, in your conflicts, it may not be the eruption, the fire, or the big event but the lingering toxic fumes that are dangerous. Sometimes, because we haven't allowed Christ to be the center of our relationships, the result is death in that relationship. If we rely on our own selfish attempts, we just keep poisoning the environment.

Flashpoints

A flashpoint occurs when the temperature in a room that's on fire gets hotter and hotter until the fire consumes all the oxygen in the room. At that point, the fire seeks out more oxygen and begins siphoning it from another room, and then that room will literally explode. These flashpoint explosions are what we see when a burning structure seems to collapse in on itself.

This happens in our conflicts as well. We have a fight, but we ignore the root cause of the conflict. We think everything's going to be okay, but it simply moves into another area of our lives and explodes. Ignoring a fire won't make it go away. James points out: "Consider what a great forest is set on fire by a small spark" (3:5).

WALKING THROUGH THE FIRE

It would be a myth and false doctrine if I were to say, "When you give your heart to Christ, you'll never have any conflicts ever again. It's just going to be *wonnnnderful*!" No, that's not necessarily true. In fact, the opposite is true. Jesus said in John 16:33, "In this world you *will* have trouble, but take heart! I have overcome the world."

Isaiah 43:2 promises, "When you walk through the fire, you will not be burned; the flames will not set you ablaze." Notice it says *when*—we are gonna walk through the fire! It's gonna happen! But our conflicts will not set us ablaze and destroy us even though we do have to go through them sometimes.

Even the apostles got into conflicts. The early disciples got into a dispute over which one was the greatest (see Luke 9:46). And in the book of Acts, a huge dispute caused a separation. Barnabas wanted to take Mark with them on a journey, but Paul was determined not to take him, since Mark had deserted them in another city. We're told, "They had such a *sharp disagreement* that they parted company. Barnabas took Mark and sailed for Cyprus, but Paul chose Silas and left, commended by the believers to the grace of the Lord" (Acts 15:39–40, emphasis added). This probably was not what God intended, but these guys got through it and God used them nonetheless.

Conflicts will always happen—they're just a consequence of living in a fallen world with people who have selfish tendencies. If they happened to the apostles, then we can count on them happening to us.

It's funny too what people will find to argue about. I once saw a video illustration of a spinning ballerina. Some people watching saw her spinning clockwise, while others saw her spinning the opposite way. People were literally arguing about which direction she was spinning! But in the end, what difference does it make? She's still spinning, right? Similarly, so many of our relational differences result from different perceptions. When we're dealing with personal perception, there doesn't have to be a wrong and a right way to view something. People looking at the same situation can see it differently.

Some differences are simple preferences, like whether or not your favorite restaurant is "the best." But some differences must be resolved before you move on. In marriage, it could be financial decisions, religious beliefs, or how to discipline your kids. Or with your business partners, it could be pricing strategies, product development, or which market to move into next. And the more differences there are, the more potential there is for conflict.

THE FIVE HATE LANGUAGES

Gary Chapman wrote a book years ago that has since become a classic, titled *The Five Love Languages*. They're well-known now: gifts, acts of service, physical touch, quality time, and encouragement. However, I'm convinced there's also a counterfeit to each one of those that gets stirred up in the heat of battle. I like to call these the "Five Hate Languages."

Instead of thinking about what we can give to help the other person, we start thinking, "What can I take from this? What's in it for me?" Rather than a gift, that's a *take*. Instead of serving others, we get on the defensive and try to "do unto them before they do unto me!" Or, even worse, we don't even bother. That's indifference, which is similar to another hate language, the opposite of quality time, which is no time. When you start thinking, "I don't have time for this," what you're essentially saying is, "I'd rather be doing something else, like watching football" (or whatever), and you retreat from your most valuable relationships. Or you could be so self-centered that spending time with others isn't even on your radar because they're not as important as you are. It happens!

How about physical touch? The opposite of physical touch is, well, physical touch. The most common type of violence in America is not stranger on stranger but between friends and family. Unforgiveness, past hurts, substance abuse, and many other circumstances can quickly turn into anger, rage, and fury. Before you know it, the situation has spiraled out of control, somebody has lost their temper, and the police are called. Rage turns into physical violence.

Instead of encouragement, when the battle heats up, we use destructive words and sarcasm. Negative words can destroy someone for years, and sometimes for a lifetime.

A good conflict can move you forward, but only if you know how to fight right. A lot of people may be good at fighting *against* each other, but they don't know how to fight *for* each other. Why?

> **A good conflict can move you forward, but only if you know how to fight right.**

Maybe it's because we don't know how to engage with each other during a conflict, so we ignore the cause—a flashpoint. Maybe we're afraid to dig around a little and figure out what's going on, or maybe we're afraid to be real about what's happening inside ourselves, so we just let the conflict smolder, hoping it'll go away. Maybe we're afraid of losing the relationship or of something more basic than that—losing face. Or maybe unforgiveness is keeping the conflict from finding resolution; it's a poison, like soot. I believe the Lord wants us to be better at fighting *for* each other, but how do we do that?

FIRE EXTINGUISHERS

Since conflict is inevitable, it takes more than just common courtesy and a few people skills to maintain healthy relationships. It takes an understanding of who the real enemy is. The Bible is very clear about this ultimate fire starter: "Be alert and of sober mind. Your enemy the devil prowls around like a roaring lion looking for someone to devour" (1 Pet. 5:8).

If only it were that easy to spot our enemy when we're in the middle of a relational conflict. Most of the time he's camouflaged. Duck hunting and deer hunting are both big in Arkansas. Around here, when you're getting ready for hunting season, you'd better have some camo! You'd better know how to move around without being noticed, or you'll miss your shot.

This is the way our enemy operates. He doesn't show up at your home hissing and wearing horns. He's manipulative, whispering little lies like "He doesn't love you like he used to" or "She's cheating on you" or "He's undermining you at the office." The Bible says he masquerades as an angel of light (see 2 Cor. 11:14).

A lot of times we think somebody else is the problem, and we conclude, "If *they* would just change, then everything would be good." During these moments we must remember, "Our struggle [our fight] is not against flesh and blood, but against the rulers, against the authorities, against the powers of this dark world and against the spiritual forces of evil in the heavenly realms" (Eph. 6:12).

This war is real. Jesus said, "The thief comes only to steal and kill and destroy; I have come that they may have life, and have it to the full" (John 10:10). The thief tries to steal your family and destroy your relationships, but Jesus said, "I came to save you from this thieving arsonist!" He offers us a way out of those little fires that our enemy wants to turn into out-of-control wildfires. Let's look at some of the ways we can fight fire with the ultimate fire extinguisher—God's power in our lives.

Recognize Your Differences

People are as different as, well, men and women! Think about it: a husband gets angry, says harsh words, thinks about it, apologizes, and then wants intimacy ten minutes later! This usually doesn't fly with his wife, which is understandable as long as you're not this particular husband.

My best friend is without a doubt my wife, Michelle. In many ways, we couldn't be more different—and I'm glad. In dating relationships, opposites attract, but in marriages, sometimes opposites attack! You have to accept that God made men and women uniquely and wonderfully different.

You also have to consider differences in personality types. If you're an extrovert, you may want to hash out the conflict immediately, but if your business partner is an introvert, he may need some time alone to calm down or think through what the problem is. He may need some space.

In most conflicts, there is one person who is the aggressor and one who is the avoider, and it's not always gender-based. The aggressor sees their pressuring behavior as promoting the health of the relationship, while the avoider sees this as control and hides until the storm is over. The aggressor is usually the big talker, while the avoider *hates* conflict and will work late hours to avoid it. The aggressor could use a lesson on contentment (see Phil. 4), while the avoider needs to learn to be more open and honest without fear. You just have to recognize and respect the differences you each bring to the relationship.

Recognize Your Responsibility

A lot of people today talk about their rights, but they forget about their calling. It's not uncommon for someone to say, "Well, *he's* the problem. I don't do everything perfectly, but he's the problem." In fact, you may say, "He's 95 percent of the problem." You may be right. He (or she) may be 95 percent of the problem. But I believe the Lord would want you to focus on *your* 5 percent, because you can't do much about the 95 percent over there. The Bible tells us, "As far as it depends on you, live at peace with everyone" (Rom. 12:18).

Did you catch that? *As far as it depends on you.* If you want to fight for people and not against them, you've gotta know that God wants you to work with him, saying with humility, "Change me, O God. Help me, O God. Lord, what is my responsibility? What is it that *I* need to change?"

This is a good opportunity for me to be transparent with you. This book is about being real, so let me be real with you about a weakness in my life. I'm ADD. My mind is constantly wandering. It's a major tendency for me. Some things that other men struggle with are not a problem for me, but I check out so easily. Knowing myself like I do, I often must remind myself to stay engaged. To focus on the person I'm with. To listen and care about what they care about. Since this is a major weakness for me, I must take responsibility for it.

It's important that we are personally devoted to finding out where it is that we're weak so we can strengthen that area first. So often what you think you're committing to in a relationship or business partnership isn't exactly what you get. That's the moment and often the season (even sometimes a lifetime) when you begin realizing that it is not the other person's responsibility to make you happy all the time.

If you want a healthy relationship, whether it's a working partnership, friendship, or marriage, you have to realize that a lot of the success depends on you! Paul encourages us: "Do nothing out of selfish ambition or vain conceit. Rather, in humility value others above yourselves, not looking to your own interests but each of you to the interests of the others" (Phil. 2:3–4).

You see, a lot of the growth in your relationships with others results from how you respond to them. As you respond to them in humility, patiently responding with kindness and enduring real and perceived injustices (because not all injustice that we experience with other people is real!), *your* responses can change *their* responses—for the better! Then you begin to learn what it means to fight for, not against, your family, your friends, your business partners.

Recognize the Presence of God

In order to put out the sparks of conflict, we often need to quit focusing on what we think we're entitled to receive in the situation and focus on God instead. Pastor Roy Stockstill, who founded the church I was on staff at for fourteen years, used to say, "A man or a woman who is on their face before the Lord will never fall from that position." It's a stable place. But think about it: We'll call our mama. We'll call a friend. We'll call a lawyer. We'll call a lot of different people before we call on God—especially in the middle of a conflict.

But God provides us with the ultimate fire extinguisher: his Holy Spirit. When Jesus left this earth, we were not abandoned—just the opposite. The Holy Spirit is called "the Comforter" and "the Helper." When you invite his presence into your conflict, he warms up the relationship somehow. It's his role! He's the one who moves about and changes us. It's why we pray, "Lord, have your way in me." We have to have the Holy Spirit.

In the middle of conflict, it's easy to ask ourselves, "What would Jesus do?" But it's much harder to actually practice what he always did. Regardless of the situation, almost always the first thing Jesus would do was look. He truly *saw* those he met. Study the way he looked at other people. He looked at the rich young ruler with love in his heart (see Mark 10:21). He saw the crowds with compassion (see Matt. 9:36). He saw the outcasts—the blind, the lepers—and he was moved with compassion to invade and change their world, even healing them completely (see Matt. 20:34; Mark 1:41). His compassion moved him to raise the widow's only son from the dead (see Luke 7:11–15). When he saw the crowds who had gathered to hear his message, his compassion moved him to feed several thousand people (more than once!) so that they could stay and hear the rest of his story, and their lives were changed forever (see Matt 14:13–21; Mark 8:1–9).

One of our pastors told me that just the other night one of his kids wanted to bless the food at dinnertime. The child started to pray, and then he started getting silly, and sillier, and then even sillier, until finally his dad looked at him and said, "You cannot pray that way. You're being silly." The kid broke down and ran to his room, sobbing. His dad went in and asked, "What did I say that hurt you so bad?" The child replied, "It's not what you said. It's the way you looked at me."

I've got that look. I can look at you and burn a hole right through you. But Jesus looked at people with compassion, and then he would speak life into their situation and even do something to bring radical change to their circumstances. This is the kind of compassion we need to draw on when we're tempted to throw gasoline on the fire of a relational conflict.

When we see a fiery situation the way God sees it, through his eyes, we begin seeing what's fueling the fire, and we start working on putting out the flames that are destroying our lives and the lives of our friends and family. This kind of compassion calls us to engage with others on a level that changes everything. Instead of reacting in anger, we should be moved by compassion to respond in love, patience, and kindness. When we respond with compassion like that, we're using fire extinguishers, and the flames die quickly.

NO SMOKING

In addition to how Jesus looked at others, the words he spoke to them reflected God's love for them. This reminds us that the language of a conflict is often more important than the content. Proverbs says, "The tongue has the power of life and death, and those who love it will eat its fruit" (18:21).

Many of the differences that start conflicts are not actually the real problem! The real problem is often the language used during the conflict. People usually forget the reason for the conflict but not the hurtful language. "Those who guard their mouths and their tongues keep themselves from calamity" (Prov. 21:23). In other words, if you want to avoid the fires, then don't start smoking!

Examples of words that will cause trouble include using the word *divorce* as a weapon in a marital fight. And how you say things is as important as what you say! Loud profanity and name-calling aren't wise choices either. "Fools vent their anger, but the wise quietly hold it back" (Prov. 29:11 NLT). When one partner explodes, the other withdraws to protect their heart. Then the one who exploded wants to blame the one who has withdrawn for not wanting to tough it out.

> The language of a conflict is often more important than the content.

Instead of this approach, learn diffusing statements, which are words you practice beforehand. In most cases, unless one person is an anger-holic, one or two soothing statements can cause the intensity of the moment to subside. "A gentle answer turns away wrath, but a harsh word stirs up anger" (Prov. 15:1). Here are some examples of diffusing statements:

- "I'm a little upset right now. Can we come back to this in an hour?"
- "It would mean so much to me if we can talk about this calmly."
- "I think the kids can hear us. Could we speak softly?"
- "The way we decide this issue is just as important as the result. Let's try to listen closely to each other."

Diffusing statements never blame the other person; they remind both people that they're in it together. On the other hand, nondiffusing statements ramp up the fight even more and add fuel to the fire. These include:

- "You always" or "You never" statements
- "Here we go again!"

- "This is just like the last time! You'll never change!"
- "I knew you'd say that—you always do!"

When we're attuned to the kind of language we're using, then we can begin using some real fire extinguishers. Here are a few of my favorite resources for true firefighting.

Fight with Encouragement

Years ago I wrote down in the back of my Bible the importance of the word *encouragement*. When we first moved to Arkansas, I was intimidated by the prospect of planting a church while knowing only one family in the whole state. The Lord reminded me, "Rick, be an encourager."

When Michelle and I are on our A game, it's always about encouragement. No one can encourage me like Michelle. I'm generally a confident person, but with Michelle? When *she* says something good about me, I feel like I can do anything! She brings to life this passage of Scripture: "If you have any encouragement from being united with Christ, if any comfort from his love, if any common sharing in the Spirit, if any tenderness and compassion, then make my joy complete by being like-minded, having the same love, being one in spirit and of one mind" (Phil. 2:1–2).

Let's look at this in the context of marriage. It's common nowadays for a man to verbally slam his wife, whether in front of her or away from her. You know what I mean, guys. You're out with the boys and you say, "I gotta go home to the old lady. You know she's gonna nag all night if I don't get home." Or, even in front of her, you throw a cheap shot. She may laugh harder than anyone else, but it's not real.

And ladies, look at your husbands. The Bible doesn't just tell a woman that she should respect her husband. Read Ephesians chapter 5. It bumps that commitment up. (That's what I like about the

Word—it always bumps it up.) It tells the wife, "You *must* respect him" (see v. 33). Why? Because God *made* that boy, and he knows that a man has to have respect. And the way that you respect your husband is with encouraging words.

Sometimes we wait for everything to be right before we encourage. But that's not the heart of God. When Jesus was being baptized, he wasn't actually doing anything. John the Baptist was doing the work, yet God the Father was talking about how proud he was of Jesus before Jesus had preached one time or done one miracle! Before he cast out a demon, before anything happened, his Father looked at him and said, "I'm proud of him."

God is the ultimate encourager. Be an encourager. Tell others how proud you are of them. The closer they are to you, the more the Lord is saying, "Be an encourager!"

Fight with Kindness

It's the *kindness* of God that leads people to repentance (see Rom. 2:4), not condemnation. I could go that route, like the Sunday school teacher I mentioned who pointed her finger at me and said, "You're going to hell, Bezet!" Is it true that if you're not born again you're going to hell? Yes, but that's not what leads people to repentance. Wouldn't it be better if I told you the truth that God wants to forgive you and that it's his kindness that put him on that cross?

What leads people to repentance is when they realize that Jesus died for *them*. I'm changed by understanding that he loves *me*! He wants me around, he's great at forgiving people, and I don't have to be down all the time. He's not holding my sin against me. He *wants* to forgive my sin!

Jesus consistently responded with kindness to those around him— sometimes even those who wanted to kill him. With lepers, he wasn't afraid to touch them and went out of his way to offer them physical touch as part of their healing (see Matt. 8:1–4). Jesus sought out a short little tax collector named Zacchaeus and said, "I'd like to have supper with you tonight—let's go!" (see Luke 19:1–10). If you look at so many of these situations, you'll see that Jesus preempted what might have been a tense or awkward situation by offering kindness. When we're being kind to someone, it's hard to keep the fires of anger, hatred, and jealousy alive.

Fight with Understanding

There are always more than two people in a conflict. What that means is that the people who have influenced your life for good or for bad have an effect on how you react. Forty percent of women and 25 percent of men have experienced physical or sexual abuse in their past. Sometimes individual counseling is needed for a person to move beyond a past negative influence. When you're in conflict with someone, it's important to understand not only the other person's position but their past experiences as well.

You also need to understand the circumstances surrounding your conflict. What pressures are influencing you both? Did something just happen that's fueling the fire? Have you had financial bad news? Has someone been drinking? Is there a medical condition? Take the time to do a personal inventory of things that might have happened that have caused you or the other person to react a certain way.

Use wisdom when you bring things up. Choose an appropriate time and manner. Fight privately! Spouses shouting at each other in front of their kids has been considered child abuse. Children do not get their sense of well-being from how much love you show them. Their security is in the fact that you *love each other*. If it's a work relationship, show the same respect for the individual by working through the conflict in private.

Don't tell details to friends. It can ruin reputations—on both sides! When you are upset, you may not care, but honor in a relationship means you cover for the other person. People will have much more respect for *you* if you cover for others. Scripture reminds us, "Above all, love each other deeply, because love covers over a multitude of sins" (1 Pet. 4:8).

Fight with Long-Suffering

Most of us don't like the word *long-suffering* because it means it takes longer than we want it to, and we'll suffer, and that's just no fun at all! The term actually means patient perseverance, and it will go a long way in bringing peace to a conflict. In practice, it means to endure the offenses of others.

It isn't necessary or even useful to constantly point out the faults of the other person, especially in conflict. They may not be in a place where they can hear it. It really is okay to let some things slide—maybe not forever, but definitely for a season. Another way of saying this is "pick your battles." It's natural to retaliate. It's not natural to opt for self-restraint. It's natural to choose self-preservation. It's not natural to favor long-suffering in the midst of conflict—but it is so good when we do.

Fight with Truth and Love

I'm a prideful person. It's hard for me to admit when I'm wrong. I've gotten a little better about it, but I know it's ridiculous that I can't be more mature than that. For example, Michelle and I would be in a state of friction about something, and I would say she's wrong, and she would respond, "No, it's this way." After it was all said and done, I would realize that I really *was* wrong, but I could barely go to her and admit it. Believe me when I say that this created a conflict within a conflict! I couldn't admit the truth, which at the time was obvious to everybody except me: *I was wrong*.

Maybe you're at a place in a conflict where you've examined your part, you've been able to find what you've done wrong, and you've been able to man up (or woman up) and admit it. Maybe you've owned your 95 percent, and now you're facing the 5 percent fault in the other person. Now what? "*Speaking the truth in love*, we will grow to become in every respect the mature body of him who is the head, that is, Christ" (Eph. 4:15, emphasis added).

You gotta have both! Speak the truth—*in love*. I'll say it this way: godly truth without love isn't godly—or truth! If you can't say whatever you need to say in love, then you don't need to say it yet. *How* you say what you say is equally important as *what* you say. And if you've gotten to a place in a conflict where you have to confront someone, look fear in the eye and tell it to take a hike so that you can tell the truth.

It's not always picture-perfect, but generally speaking, when I have reached a point where I have to confront somebody about their mistake, I wrap everything I say in love, support, and encouragement for the other person, so much so that they actually feel encouraged by the confrontation. Why? Because when it's over, it's over! I briefly explain what they did wrong, I show them how they can fix the problem, and then *I move past it.*

You can too! It's called *forgiveness*. Here's where we have an opportunity to practice pursuing the heart of God in the midst of a conflict, and then like God, we can choose to focus on the future. Don't think about it anymore. You addressed it. Move on.

As we've seen, the fires of conflict are always going to spring up in the midst of our relationships. However, we don't have to try to avoid these or win these or become anything less than genuine in order to turn these potentially destructive sparks into constructive opportunities. We simply have to be real, open, and honest. We rely on the example of Jesus, the love of our heavenly Father, and the power of his Holy Spirit dwelling in us.

9

BE NOT AFRAID

Overcoming Paralyzing Fear

When I was in ninth grade, I was getting pretty good at golf and got into my first playoff at Briarwood Country Club. I was especially nervous about playing one particular guy because he was a senior and he was really good. Arriving at the clubhouse, I was so anxious that I could hardly breathe. My dad wasn't able to be there, and I felt all alone. And I definitely felt intimidated by my opponent and suspected that he would be able to see it on my face.

I tried to act cool and laid-back, like I wasn't nervous at all. We flipped a coin and I lost, so I had to hit first. I went up to the tee box and teed up the ball. When I took the club back, I became so tense that I got a charley horse in my leg. So during my backswing, with pain shooting up my calf, I screamed all the way around, "Aaahhhhhhh!" I completed my swing, screaming and yelling, and as I looked up, I saw that I had hit the longest drive I had ever hit in my life, dead straight down the center. I couldn't believe it!

As I was watching this amazing fluke, I also realized that everyone around us was laughing at me. Then I thought, "Maybe they're just impressed!" So I just started acting like I was good. I picked up the tee and strutted over to the side. Then my opponent got up there, and I don't know if it was because I intimidated him, but I do know he hit his ball out of bounds!

FEAR NOT

No matter how comfortable we are with ourselves or how many accomplishments we've racked up, nearly everyone gets intimidated by other people sooner or later. It may be feeling nervous when forced to make a presentation at work. Or it can be that tightening of the gut that occurs when your boss calls you in for a one-on-one meeting. Maybe it's talking with strangers or meeting new people in your small group at church. The problem is that in order to be real, we need authentic self-confidence—not arrogance or smugness but a genuine sense of our true selves that we bring to every situation. We need confidence in who God made us to be.

There's no greater authenticity killer and confidence kidnapper than fear. Feeling afraid erodes our sense of being okay with who we are, the way God made us. We end up feeling threatened, overwhelmed, inadequate, weak, and even powerless. When we're afraid, we act defensively and end up doing and saying things that don't reflect who we really are. Like my experience in the golf tournament, we often try to hide our fear and "fake it," cultivating a mask to hide behind. Sometimes it may even work, but over time we end up trying to be something or someone that's not our true selves.

> **In order to be real, we need authentic self-confidence.**

Almost everyone suffers from a fear of something: fear of failure, fear of snakes, fear of insects, fear of commitment, and so on. Not many people realize that I fight a fear, but let me tell you, I have been absolutely terrified of heights. Roller coasters do not bother me, and I am totally fearless on any theme park ride. However, walk me near a steep cliff, and you are going to have a real problem!

A few years back, I was with two of my executive pastors in Ireland, and we made the trip to the beautiful Cliffs of Moher. My friends walked up to the cliffs, within about five feet from the edge, and I couldn't take it. I began screaming at them, "Get away from that edge! If you want to get that close you have to crawl like a snake!" They realized how desperately serious I was and complied with my request, but they have not allowed me to live it down since.

I'm convinced one fear in particular undermines our healthy self-confidence and ability to be real. The Bible calls it the "fear of man" and makes it clear that when we succumb to it, we're not fully trusting in God. Proverbs tells us, "Fear of man will prove to be a snare, but whoever trusts in the LORD is kept safe" (29:25).

Fear of man is the main barrier that stops us from relating authentically to people, especially those we perceive to be successful. Be honest: if Bill Gates came to your house to talk to you, you might be a little intimidated! Maybe you wouldn't be able to think straight. Being yourself? Well, forget that!

You might have a hard time because you would be trying to make a good impression on one of the wealthiest and most successful human beings on the planet. That is the fear of man. Essentially, you're elevating someone else's opinion of you above what God thinks of you. God created you to be yourself, unique and special and unlike anyone else. The fear of man also elevates someone else above you, as if he or she were somehow better or more valuable or more important than you are. This is nothing but a lie from our enemy. In fact, every inordinate fear is based on his lies and distortions.

Fear of man is particularly evil, however, for two reasons. First, it places a person or people above God in importance. Second, it makes us unequal in the eyes of God, when we are all created in God's image and are equally loved by him. It can begin when we are children, afraid to raise our hand in class. What if our answer is wrong? The kids will laugh at us. The teacher might make fun of us. What if our answer is right? The kids may not like us anymore because they will think we are trying to impress the teacher. Nothing's worse than a "teacher's pet"!

If you realize that you are nervous or uptight around certain people you see as successful and you are afraid to even encourage them, then there's no way you are going to share the Good News of

Jesus Christ with them or pray for them or be your real self around them. This is why you have to get free of the fear of man—and you can be. As the psalmist reminds us, "The LORD is my light and my salvation—whom shall I fear? The LORD is the stronghold of my life—of whom shall I be afraid?" (27:1).

A LITTLE RESPECT

Fear of people you misperceive as better than you are shows them the wrong kind of respect, because you elevate them so much that you see yourself as nothing compared to them. What's worse, you take God completely out of the picture. All you see is the great person, and you give them total power over you. Whatever they say, you agree with them. Whatever they tell you to do, you do it. In a practical sense, whether you realize it or not, you have made them your god.

This kind of reverence is not showing real respect to the successful person. If you respected them from God's perspective, you would see yourself as just as important as they are in the eyes of God, and your standard for success would be God, not them. Jesus told us to love others as we love ourselves (see Mark 12:31). It stands to reason that you will respect others as you respect yourself too. The fear of man disappears when you show people the same respect God shows you and everyone else in the world. But it took one particular encounter in one special relationship to reveal this to me.

Only one person ever really caused me to exhibit symptoms of the fear of man, and that was Pastor Larry Stockstill. My fear was based on how much respect I had for his godly leadership and example. I worked with him and for him for nearly fourteen years, and I have never seen anyone raise up leaders better than he does. I often refer to him as a Spirit-filled General Patton, because he is forceful in nature and walks with genuine authority. Rarely, if ever, was there any reason for him to be firm with me, because I worked hard to produce what he expected from a pastor under his leadership.

Then God began to mess with me. He stirred my heart about planting a church on my own, and I knew I had to tell Pastor Larry about it. So one day I sucked in my gut, walked into his office, and casually mentioned to him that I had something I wanted to talk with him about. He asked me on the spot, "What is it?"

I shrunk back. "Well, we don't have to talk about it right now, just sometime in the next few weeks."

He replied, "Okay. Our boys play baseball together today; I'll meet you by the ball field."

I smiled and said, "Great, see you then." But I thought, *Oh great! Today?* I immediately began to pray for the game to be rained out, but God won't answer that kind of prayer!

So I went to the game as planned and saw Pastor Larry standing exactly where he had promised. He asked, "What's on your mind, Rick?"

I told him God had given me a desire to plant a church and I wanted his input. He quickly came back with, "This is not a good time. We have just opened our new campus, and I need you to help me." His words were as strong and definitive as ever, and he was not open to a rebuttal.

This moment presented a crossroads for me, and by God's grace I was able to choose the right direction. Had fear prevailed, I would have walked away without communicating my heart, with my hopes dashed, or even feeling offended. Instead, I was able to tell him, "Pastor Larry, I didn't come here to tell you what I was going to do or when I was going to do it. I came to let you hear what is on my heart. I will wait until you think it is as good an idea as I do."

In that definitive moment, I respected myself as much as I respected Pastor Larry. I respected the call God had placed on my heart as much as I respected the call God had placed on Pastor Larry's heart. I overcame any fear of man through a godly respect for myself and for another man of God. As a result, over one year later Pastor Larry said to me, "I can tell this dream is not dying inside of you. You can start looking for the city where God will send you to plant a church."

Through this experience I realized my life and calling are just as important and significant to God as anyone else's life and calling. This revelation didn't make me arrogant; it made me humble. Before, I always believed in showing respect to everyone, but now I know the truth behind that belief: I must respect myself and who God made me and called me to be *first*, and then I will show the right respect to others. I will not fear man, because I fear God.

THERE'S NO COMPARISON

An interesting dynamic comes into play for some people when it comes to respect. Sometimes it's easier for Christians to respect ordinary people than the successful ones they encounter at work, at church, or in their communities. Curiously enough, the person who is down and out appreciates being respected, but many people, especially those who work hard to be successful, *expect* it. If the way into a man's heart is through food, the way into a successful person's trust is through respect. I have also found that most successful people have strong personalities and are often suspicious of people trying to take advantage of them. Genuine, godly respect disarms this suspicion and puts them at ease.

When I visit the business of a church member, I automatically look for things to compliment, like a polite staff, a neat warehouse, a peaceful environment, or an accomplishment or award on display. I usually ask questions like, "Where do you find such great people? How much training does it take to cause them to be so motivated?" Not only am I genuinely interested, but I also want to honor them for what they are doing. Being a businessperson is also a calling from God.

Success can be seen in less obvious ways. When Michelle and I visit the home of a family with kids who are excelling and well behaved, we realize it took successful parenting to accomplish this. Whether the children do well in academics, sports, or some other area, their achievements and godly attitudes were not an accident. It is our goal to honor the family for what they have accomplished, which is rarely done in our time and culture.

In reaching out to people, it is important that we not compare ourselves to them. If we look at whatever they have and compare it to what we have, we can't encourage them. Believe me, people can smell envy a mile away! The goal is for us to be real and respectful no matter who we encounter, whether it's a billionaire or a beggar.

The apostle Paul addressed the issue of comparison in strong terms. "We do not dare to classify or compare ourselves with some who commend themselves. When they measure themselves by themselves and compare themselves with themselves, they are not wise" (2 Cor. 10:12). God is basically saying, "Don't compare yourself with others, because you'll find somebody who's better than you and you'll be discouraged, or you'll find somebody who stinks and then pride will take over and you'll think, 'Well, at least I'm way better than they are!'"

Instead of comparing yourself, look for ways to show respect and honor to all people you come in contact with. Treat them the way Jesus would treat them. Treat them the way you would like to be treated yourself—nothing less than the Golden Rule. With this mind-set, you will find that any trouble you have had with fear of man quickly melts away. The only godly comparison is between you and Jesus, and the only godly competition is with yourself—to become more and more like Jesus.

BIG SHOES TO FILL

In addition to fear of man, another poison that corrodes our self-confidence is living by logic and not by faith. When we start second-guessing other people's responses, their motives, and their reactions, we're basically back to trying to manipulate them. We're not trusting God enough to be real and let others respond accordingly. When the stakes are high—say, with a promotion at work or a special relationship—it's tempting to overthink and try to make others react the way we want them to. This seems to happen when we rely only on surface evidence, appearances, and assumptions. You know what they say happens when we assume things!

We see this illustrated when Moses sent twelve spies into Canaan to see if they could take the Promised Land (see Num. 13). They went in to scout it, analyze it, and study it intellectually. And that became a big part of their problem! Intellectualism interrupts your faith, every time. When they went in, they saw enemy nations and giants in the land and all concluded, "We're gonna die!"—all except for

Intellectualism interrupts your faith.

two people, and Joshua was one of them. Joshua was confident, because of his faith in God, that something was going to change. He didn't want it to be just another year wandering around in the desert.

Joshua also knew he had big sandals to fill—those of Moses, who had led the nation out of Pharaoh's captivity in Egypt. Just to give us a little perspective, notice that before the story of Joshua, told in the book of Joshua, you have the book of Deuteronomy. The very last verse in that book shows what God Almighty says about Moses, who has died and has to be replaced. Look at what Deuteronomy 34:12 says: "For no one has ever shown the mighty power or performed the awesome deeds that Moses did in the sight of all of Israel." That includes all his peers. Everyone.

I find it very interesting that since Moses was credited with writing the book of Deuteronomy, Moses could possibly have written that verse about himself. Regardless of whether it was Moses who wrote it, or Joshua, or someone else, it wasn't in there because it was just one man's idea! No, God agreed to it. It was truth, which is why it made the cut into the Book of Truth. Moses *was* the most powerful person who had ever lived. He *was* amazing. All of Israel knew it. So when God approached Joshua to lead the Israelites, Joshua was intimidated, because he was comparing himself to Moses. Imagine that.

Joshua had been a person of incredible confidence. He had been one of the two spies who saw the giants as grasshoppers and said, "We could take 'em!" He was a person with swagger. But by this point he'd lost it. That can happen to us too. Just because you had confidence last year doesn't mean you'll have it this year. Just because you used to have the faith to lead, you were spiritually strong, and people admired you doesn't mean that it stays that way.

God says to Joshua, "Have I not commanded you? Be strong and courageous. Do not be afraid; do not be discouraged, for the LORD your God will be with you wherever you go" (Josh. 1:9–10). Whatever you do, you're not alone! Look, God is not trying to make you feel comfortable; he's working on your character. God says, "I'll go with you. We can change some things. We can get this done!"

Another reason why I think Joshua was intimidated was that the assignment was epic. God was telling Joshua that he wanted him to do great things. He didn't end the dream of great accomplishments with Moses. What God was asking Joshua to do was incredible. Huge! And it will be incredible for you as well, if you will listen to the voice that says, "Give me some time. Be with me in devotion. I know your life is hectic, but if you battle by working harder, it won't be enough, and you'll get distracted, worried, and upset." You'll be intimidated when you take your focus off God and put it on what he's giving you to do. You'll be tempted to stop living by faith and begin living by what you can see, by what seems logical.

Please get this. Anytime the Lord asks you to do something, it's not going to be a piece of cake. It's always going to be huge. The Lord is asking me to do some things this year to make my marriage better. I don't want to do them! But I know it's worth it. Everything God asks us to do is a huge challenge, and it's worth it.

CONFIDENCE BUILDERS

So how can we overcome these barriers that threaten our self-confidence and our faith—along with our ability to be real? How can we build our confidence in a healthy way that relies on God and liberates us to be real? I believe we begin by conditioning ourselves to filter every circumstance through God's promises. For instance, consider this amazing promise he gives us in John: "I have told you these things, so that in me you may have peace. In this world you will have trouble. But take heart! I have overcome the world" (16:33).

Maybe you'll think this is weird, but because of this promise, I actually look forward to crisis. Why? Because I know it's going to come anyway, and it gives me the opportunity to see it the way God does. Somebody has accused me of seeing positive in *every* circumstance, and I do!

I have seen couples come to me for marriage counseling, mad at each other with passionate rage. I tell them, "You are mad at each other because you have such passion." They leave feeling like they have passion—*for* each other. It works.

God has given us many promises in his Word. Use a search tool and find them. You will be amazed at what God promises—to you! Keep his promises in front of you, and tell God you believe them. Based on these promises and the truth of God's Word, here are a few important ideas to remember in order to remain self-confident, faithful, and real.

It's Not about Winning

We're told in Philippians, "Do nothing out of selfish ambition or vain conceit. Rather, in humility value others above yourselves" (2:3). The word for "selfish ambition" in the Greek means "competitive." So it's saying, "Don't be competitive around each another." Basically, we're not to compare and we're also not to compete. It's really tough to cooperate on a real level with other people when we fall into either of these two traps.

Do you know how many people are competitive? Have you ever watched a quarterback who's competing against his own wide receiver? Ask Terrell Owens if it's ever happened! Of course it has happened, and it still does. The problem is that when you start getting competitive, like Shaq and Kobe did during their day, you start thinking more about yourself than others. And it's a big mess. They were able to win, but the more competitive they got, the harder it got for them to play together, and Shaq left.

A husband will say, "I'm the one working the hardest around here." And the wife will shoot back, "I'm the one spending the most time with the kids." "Yeah, well, you don't bring as much money in here as I do." "Well, the kids like me more than they like you." On and on it goes! Back and forth! Competitive instead of cooperative.

Some friends of mine were having dinner at a restaurant with an arguing couple. It got awkward. The man reached his limit and said, "I don't understand. How did God make you so beautiful but so stupid?"

She responded, "Well, he made me beautiful so you would be attracted to me, and he made me stupid so I would be attracted to *you*!"

Please get this: you are not the most important person, especially in your house. And guys especially, the bigger role you have at work, the harder it is to swallow this idea. At the wedding, they stand up for the bride, not you. The most important person in your home is not you. It's the people you serve.

Show Interest in Others, Even When You Don't Feel Like It

Jesus knew we would forget this, so he set the precedent. He washed feet. He even said one time, "Look, I did not come for you to serve me. I came to serve you!" (see Mark 10:45). So Jesus washed the disciples' feet. Even Judas's feet! Why? Of course he knew their feet were dirty. Everybody had dirty feet back then. They wore sandals and they walked on dirt roads. But that's not why he washed their feet. He did it because it was an act of humility to wash someone else's feet. He was trying to show them that they weren't the most important people around.

We're told, "Each of you should look not only to your own interests, but also to the interests of others" (Phil. 2:4 NIV 1984). This is not very deep, but I'll say it: I find that I am interested in the things that I am interested in! If I'm not interested in something, I'm not interested in it. That's why this Scripture says to be interested in one another, not in your own interests.

My wife doesn't like golf. I know the truth: she hates it. But if I start talking about it, she listens. I'll say, "Baby, that's Phil Mickelson right there. He's a golfer, and his wife had cancer," and she'll say, "Oh, really?" With some context of people's lives and what they're facing, she gets into it. If I go play golf, she wants to know what I shot. She acts like she cares. Maybe she's even starting to like it.

She likes theater, so I'll go. Forgive me, but *Phantom of the Opera*? Talk about "Music of the Night"—oh my goodness, I fell asleep! But she wanted to go and absolutely loved it. And because I love her, I was happy to go. I try hard to be interested in what she's interested in, even though it's not my thing.

Practice Patience, Especially with Annoying People

Sometimes taking an interest in others can stretch your patience to the limit. Several years ago when my golf game was steadily climbing, my wife set me up to play at a very exclusive golf resort. I found out later that the starter had placed me with the wrong group. When I walked up to meet them, a man with a rough, gravelly voice glared at me. "Boy, you aren't supposed to play with us." It was obvious by the way this guy—let's call him Don—carried himself that he was successful, and he was definitely confrontational. He continued to challenge me. "You want to bet on the match?"

"No thanks," I said politely. I knew Don was wealthy, and I probably could have taken him for a million or so, but being a pastor puts definite limitations on how you receive offerings! As we played, it was obvious that Don was the main man in this group. The other two guys laughed at his crude jokes, and I was becoming more and more irritated. When Don cracked another nasty joke, I just stared at him with no intention of looking away until one of us broke. He looked away first. *Yes!* My point was made.

We finished the game, I said good-bye, and I walked away. Then I heard Don calling after me, "Boy, hold up there! I wanna talk to you." He got in my face and rudely demanded, "Are you a *Christian*?"

Aggravated, I wanted to say, "The name's *Bezet. Rick Bezet.*" But I answered firmly, "Yes sir, I'm a Christian." I started to go on, but he wouldn't let me talk, even after he asked me something.

"Shut up, boy. Are you a preacher?"

I nodded.

"Look, boy, I used to walk with God, but now I'm away from him. I admire you and think you're a good man." Then he actually let me speak long enough to pray with him to rededicate his life. He even brought me back over to the other golfers and told them, "Look, this man is a preacher, and I like him." He slapped me on the shoulder and said, "You can go now, boy!" I didn't know whether to be relieved or even angrier!

> **Successful people need encouragement just like anybody else.**

After my experience with Don, I discovered that successful people need encouragement just like anybody else. Many wealthy people grew up in broken homes or poverty, dealt with alcoholic parents, or had some great obstacle to overcome. Others may have been raised in a nearly perfect atmosphere, yet they still have the basic human need to be affirmed for who they are and not what they do or how much money they have.

Everyone needs encouragement! Successful people are different because their needs generally do not scream at you. Like Don, they wait until they find a person they respect and trust, someone who understands them and cares enough to meet them where they feel most comfortable. Then they will open up, and you will find they are really a lot like you.

Courageously Step Out in Faith

God had to tell Joshua in Joshua 1 to be "strong and courageous" three times before it finally began to sink in! But God's patient perseverance in building up Joshua as the new leader paid off. Finally, Joshua, who had been intimidated before, got up, looked at everybody, and said, "Hey! Today is going to be amazing! Today we're going into the Promised Land. For forty years we've missed this, but not today! Today is different. The very thing that God has always wanted for all of us? Today we're going to get it. Today. Get up and let's go!"

That day was Joshua's today, but this can be *your* today! I highly recommend that you get alone with your family and tell them, "Today is going to be different. As for me and my house, we're going to serve the Lord. Today." The times are just too crazy for us to spend another year just wandering aimlessly. Today is a day of salvation. Today.

You may be more confident that your best days are behind you or that you have ruined your life than you are confident that God is working on something in you that is really good. When you hit the golf ball outside of the fairway, sometimes the rough is intense and all you can do is chip it back onto the fairway to start again. If you need a reroute, sometimes all you can do is get back into play. I promise you, though, when you get back into the zone of God, it's awesome! To hear from the Lord is amazing.

The Holy Spirit still speaks today. Scripture says, "Being confident of this, that he who began a good work in you will carry it on to completion" (Phil. 1:6). He is able to do it. Now that's a confidence you can count on—not being confident in who you are or what you can do, but being confident that God's got this!

This confidence in God and his sovereignty is the source of true self-confidence. It's what allows us to let go of having to fear others, try to manipulate them, or rely strictly on what our senses tell us. If we want to be real, then we have to understand that God is our power source. He's in control and has our best interests at heart. That, my friend, will make you confident, faithful, and real.

10

ROCK SOLID

Being Real with Confidence

One day my wife, Michelle, asked me to go to the store to pick up a few items, and of course on the list was a certain feminine product. Now, this is every man's worst nightmare, and perhaps for a mature, responsible, loving husband, it's his worst nightmare because it's hard to say no. So being the mature, responsible, loving husband that I am, I reluctantly agreed, threw on a ball cap and sunglasses, headed into the store, and casually strolled toward the necessary aisle. The entire time I kept praying, "Lord, please don't let me see anyone from church. Just this once, let me get out of here without anyone noticing me."

With focused effort, I managed to find the right product and did my best to hide it among the other items on my list, as well as a few that weren't, just to make sure no one could see the pink box peeking out. I got the last thing on my list and headed toward the checkout line, about to let out a sigh of relief and say a prayer of thanksgiving—too soon. Just as I stepped into line, I slipped on a wet spot on the floor.

My arms went up in the air, the basket I was holding and everything in it flew high above me, and I fell to the ground in what seemed like slow motion. The fall on my back was so hard that it took a minute or so for me to catch my breath, and I saw people pointing and laughing in my direction. "Okay, Lord," I thought, "now would be a really good time for you to hook me up with the rapture." However, nobody offered to help me up, which both annoyed and relieved me at the same time.

I considered getting up and running out of the store, driving across town to another store, and starting all over again. But as I sat there for another minute, a smile began to form on my face. Surely I had enough confidence as a man to handle a little accident—feminine products, sore back, and all—and get up and keep going. So I did just that. Somehow I managed to get up, collect my things (including a lovely pink box), and get through the checkout line without dying. By the time I was in my car on the way home, I was laughing at myself.

My momentary loss of manly confidence reminded me of a story I'd heard about the late Sam Walton, the founder of Walmart, whose international headquarters are here in Arkansas. Mr. Walton had opened his first retail store in Newport, Arkansas. He wanted to build the best general merchandise store in town, and he was very successful—so much so that his landlord wanted the location for himself and found a way to squeeze Sam Walton out of the business.

At the time there was no other place to go shopping in that small town. Sam Walton later said it was the low point in his business life, truly like a nightmare. (I'm assuming he never had to buy a certain product for his wife!) He was not down for long, though, and we all know the rest of the story. If he had lost hope in God and confidence in himself, no one would know who he was. But he didn't. Sam Walton remembered who he was, got back on his feet, and found another way to move toward his life's calling.

BUILDING BRIDGES

We all have those incidents, both small (like my embarrassing fall in the checkout line) and large (like Mr. Walton's loss of his business location), that leave us lying on the floor feeling ambushed by life. Maybe it comes when our credit card is declined at the restaurant or when we don't get the promotion that had been promised to us. It could be discovering our spouse's list of favorite online sites or finding out a trusted friend betrayed our confidence.

Our first response may be to run and hide, to put on a mask, to pretend we're not hurt or disappointed. But these moves usually don't help us be more authentic people and grow in our confidence. As we'll see, trusting in God and getting back on our feet is the only way to move forward.

No matter what occupation you decide to pursue or what type of relationship you involve yourself in, you must have confidence in order to be authentic and fulfilled in your life. A sense of confidence will improve the way people relate to you. You will be more productive, more loving, more secure, and even better looking (really!) if confidence is strong in you. You will be a better spouse, better friend, better employee, and better parent if healthy confidence is alive at the core of your being.

The problem I find with a majority of people today is that they have a dangerously low level of confidence. It's a condition present in Christians and non-Christians alike. The kind of confidence I'm talking about isn't just the personal motivation, self-help, you-can-do-it kind that you might get from watching an *Oprah* rerun or listening in on a coach's halftime locker room speech. No, I'm talking about something deeper and longer lasting.

True confidence is a spiritual quality.

You see, I believe that true confidence is a spiritual quality that fundamentally affects how we see the world, each other, ourselves, and God. The author of Hebrews says, "Now faith is *confidence* in what we hope for and assurance about what we do not see" (11:1, emphasis added). The word here that we translate as "confidence" is *hupostasis*, which literally means the supporting structure, the basis for something, our assurance or strong understanding. It's the power under something that provides a foundation for what's above it.

This definition helps explain why I see confidence as being an essential quality in one's soul. Like the girders that support the Lake Pontchartrain Causeway Bridge down in my friend Boudreaux's neck of the woods near N'awlins, our confidence supports our life's journey. And if you've ever driven across that bridge—the longest in the world at almost twenty-four miles!—then you know you want complete faith that it will support you all the way across. Your confidence should build bridges in your life that last for the long haul.

Paul's not the only one writing about confidence in the Bible; it's used in both the Old and New Testaments dozens of times. Let's look at a few other verses where God's Word reminds us about the importance of confidence:

> For you have been my hope, Sovereign LORD,
>   my confidence since my youth. (Ps. 71:5)

> But blessed is the one who trusts in the LORD,
>   whose confidence is in him. (Jer. 17:7)

> So do not throw away your confidence; it will be richly rewarded. (Heb. 10:35)

> This is the confidence we have in approaching God: that if we ask anything according to his will, he hears us. (1 John 5:14)

In the first verse above, the word *confidence* is a noun referring to the Lord. He is your confidence. Like a rock, he's always there for you. In the later two verses found in the New Testament, the word means "freedom to speak openly" or "cheerful courage." It reminds me of when my kids were little and they would come running up and jump in my lap, and then we'd have a ticklefest or go get ice cream. They weren't afraid to approach me. They didn't feel like they had to make an appointment, because I'm their dad.

RUNNING ON EMPTY

If confidence is so vital to our well-being, then why is it so hard to hold on to? If anything, as Christians we should be more confident than anyone else. Yet our confident foundation seems to crack and wash away in life's storms faster than a mobile home in a hurricane. Without real confidence, we usually end up faking it by default. Our integrity, which I'm defining as the ability to experience wholeness in Christ, suffers. If our foundation has cracks in it, then we can't expect the house to be very sturdy.

I believe people struggle with self-confidence for several reasons. Often it's because we don't receive the proper fuel we need to keep our emotional "tanks" full. After our relationship with God, which we've explored, our families should be the place where we fill up. But in many cases they become the place where we're always running on empty, pouring out to others, holding up the bridge for our spouse, kids, and aging parents.

Husbands are often afraid to be vulnerable with their wives for fear of being weak, when in fact it demonstrates great trust and strength. Wives work hard to be all things to all people and lose sight of who they are in the midst of housekeeping, carpooling, working late, and starting early. Even our kids these days feel pressured to perform, to not just play sports but to win so they can get a scholarship to a good college, to not only make good grades but to be first in their class.

After our families, we all need close friends who love and support us. Unfortunately, friends have become a numbers game on Facebook, not a source of relationships in which we're loved and challenged and valued for who we are. Too many of us have been betrayed by close friends and find it hard to open up our hearts to trust again. So we hide behind our social media sites and our texts, carefully insulating ourselves from what we long for most—intimate friendships with people who know us and love us for who we are and not just what we can do for them.

Churches, instead of being a reliable cure for low confidence, have often contributed to the problem. They can be places to compare and compete, to hide and conform, rather than communities of men and women loving God and following Christ together. Instead of strengthening our soul's confidence, they leave us weaker and afraid to be genuinely hopeful—just the opposite of what God intended.

CONFIDENT CHRISTIANS

With our tanks running low, especially in places and relationships where they should be filled, it's vitally important for you to know that God is dedicated to building you up. He wants your foundation to be rock solid in him so that you are free to be real. Knowing the truth about how God sees you and how he wants to encourage and strengthen you will change your confidence level in so many ways. Let's check out a few of them.

We Have Confidence in God's Amazing Grace

I heard an amazing point in a message recently regarding Peter and Judas. There was little difference between the sins that these two disciples committed. One denied; one betrayed. Both followed and claimed to love their Master but then let him down in the clutch.

Peter boasted about how much he loved Jesus and would stand by him, and then he said he never knew him—not once but three times—just a few hours later (see Matt. 26:35, 69–75)! With Judas, whether he succumbed to greed for money or jealousy over the attention the Messiah attracted or something else, we don't know. But we do know that after he handed over Jesus to the Jewish officials for thirty pieces of silver, he couldn't live with himself and gave up hope (see Matt. 26:14–16; 27:1–5).

> **Knowing the truth about how God sees you and how he wants to encourage and strengthen you will change your confidence level.**

183

After Jesus rose from the dead, an angel told the women, "Go, tell his disciples and Peter" (Mark 16:7). Why single out Peter? Because he had failed, and God wanted his confidence restored. I believe that if Judas had been alive as well, the angel would have said, "Go, tell the disciples and Peter, and get Judas too."

God is into restoring our confidence. "Let us then approach God's throne of grace *with confidence*, so that we may *receive mercy* and *find grace* to help us in our time of need" (Heb. 4:16, emphasis added).

We Have Confidence in Approaching Him as Father

The way we approach God has a lot to do with building and sustaining our level of confidence. He makes it very clear throughout his Word how he wants us to relate to him: "For you did not receive the spirit of bondage again to fear, but you received the Spirit of adoption by whom we cry out, 'Abba, Father'" (Rom. 8:15 NKJV). He's not a judge waiting to condemn us or a traffic cop trying to catch us flying down the road. He's not an impartial observer we pass by on the street. He's our *Daddy*.

Far from shouting and berating us, God addresses us as his children, created in his image. He knows us intimately, down to the number of hairs on our head—although for some of us, he doesn't have to count very high! Some people even say he is a whisperer, that he has a still, small voice so that we have to be close to him in order to hear.

Now, this is definitely not like my family—the Bezets are a loud bunch! We talk loud; we laugh loud; we eat loud and cry loud. Except for my youngest child, Grace. She is a whisperer. There are times when we have people over and are making lots of noise in the house, and Grace will come to me to say something. "What, Grace? What?" I will have to lean in and get my ear really close to her mouth to hear what she wants to say. It's usually something like, "I just wanted to say hello," which always makes me smile.

Yes, God whispers so we will get close enough to listen. He may have our attention because of a dramatic event or painful circumstance, but when he speaks, it's usually quietly. "After the earthquake a fire, but the LORD was not in the fire; and after the fire a still small voice" (1 Kings 19:12 NKJV).

Even when we've blown it and he'd have every right to "give us the what for," as my dad used to say, God reaches out to us with wide-open arms. We all know the story of the prodigal son—how after losing everything he decided he wanted to go home to his father (see Luke 15:11–32). If he was like me when I was younger and missed curfew, he probably rehearsed a speech to give when he got there. But it never happened! His father saw him from far off and rushed to greet him in celebration. He never got to the speech, because his father's love overwhelmed him.

> **God whispers so we will get close enough to listen.**

When my oldest son, Hunter, was around five years old, I took him fishing. I told him for sure we were going to catch a fish. But he didn't care at all; he was busy throwing rocks and sticks and playing in the mud. All the while, I was anxiously trying to catch a fish and finally got one. While he wasn't looking, I took the fish off my hook and put it on his. "Hunter, come look! I think the Lord has shown me you are going to catch a fish."

The next day I asked him to tell Michelle about our trip. I said, "Hunter, tell your mom if we caught anything."

He said, "Yeah, Dad caught a fish, put it on my line, and let me catch it." I asked him why he didn't tell me he knew what I did, and he gave me a great response: "Because I was just having a good time being with you."

God wants us to enjoy spending time with him, and he has paid a hefty price for us to have that privilege. As a result, we can have more confidence toward him than we ever thought possible.

We Have Confidence to Look Forward

When we catch on to how much God loves us, we also understand more clearly the unique purpose he's given us. Like Sam Walton, who refused to accept defeat when he lost his first store's lease, we grow in confidence to conquer life's obstacles and annihilate the works of the enemy. We gain confidence knowing God's plans for us and refuse to give up, no matter how impossible his plans may seem.

Now, I believe there are four categories of dreams we can have: no dreams, low dreams, the wrong dreams, and God's dreams. We often settle for the first three and lose sight of the only dream worth pursuing, the only one that will fulfill us and bring us the joyful, abundant life Jesus told us he came to bring.

It's tempting to allow our dreams to be limited by our past mistakes and wrong turns. We end up so worried about what we've done and the limitations of the consequences we now face that we lose sight of where we're going. This "backwards vision" reminds me of what I experience in my wife's car. Whenever I get into Michelle's car to drive, I find the mirrors are pointed to the sky, the ground, and anywhere but the right direction!

I'll tell her, "Use the mirrors—they're paid for!" But she replies, "I don't need them because I'm not driving backwards—I'm going forward." Now, this is not a good driving technique, but it's a great principle for pursuing God's dreams. As we're reminded by Paul, we keep the confidence we have in our dreams by "forgetting what is behind and straining toward what is ahead" (Phil. 3:13).

We Have Confident Boldness

Following Jesus is a blast if you decide not to be intimidated by people. So many Christians I know are intimidated by others, and I think this frustrates God. They're afraid that others will reject, abandon, or outright hurt them. We see this when Jesus was teaching his disciples about the cost of following him and openly speaking about his Father. Christ made it clear that there will be times of persecution. He challenged the disciples not to fear men who opposed them. "Don't be afraid of those who want to kill your body; they cannot touch your soul" (Matt. 10:28 NLT).

God consistently reminds us that our confidence does not come from what people think of us but comes from our relationship with him. This may explain why I love these verses in Hebrews so much: "God has said, 'Never will I leave you; never will I forsake you.' So we say with confidence, 'The Lord is my helper; I will not be afraid. What can mere mortals do to me?'" (13:5–6).

Many people never make a phone call to restore a relationship because of fear. Some people have not ventured out to start that new business because they're afraid. Others can't bring themselves to tell their spouse the truth and ask for forgiveness, for the same reason. Using the responses of others as the source of your confidence will never work for long. You end up relationally and emotionally paralyzed when you live your life trying to please people. You become afraid to take risks and be yourself. So you run and hide your real self again.

But when you let go of what other people think and remember what God thinks, you discover the wonderful freedom to speak the truth, even when it's risky. Once while shopping in a local 7-Eleven convenience store, I saw a man drop a carton of milk, then with a loud, angry voice yell, "Jesus Christ!" Feeling bold that day, I told him, "Man, why don't you yell out 'Buddha!' or 'Hare Krishna!' or something? But please don't use Jesus's name that way." When I got to the counter, the employee smiled and told me in his Cajun accent, "Dat Buddha ting, dat was really good!"

You may remember the story of the rich young ruler (see Mark 10). The Bible says that the man actually "ran" to Jesus, fell on his knees, and asked, "What must I do to inherit eternal life?" (v. 17). Jesus told him to keep the law, which the man said he had done since

> **Because God accepts us, we have the confidence to be real.**

he was young. Then Jesus gave him one more instruction that involved a big sacrifice, but the man decided not to do it. It was a risk he simply didn't have the confidence to take. Perhaps he thought, "What will others think of me if I give everything to the poor? How will they know I'm important?" So instead, he walked away depressed and discouraged.

We don't know the man's name or anything else about him. A single act of obedience would have caused his name to be known throughout the centuries in the most powerful book ever written. Jesus had confidence toward all people, and I am certain he would love for us to have it too.

We Have Confident Authenticity

As we've explored over the past nine chapters, God wants all of us, just the way we are, open and honest. Because he accepts us, we have the confidence to be real. To come out of hiding for good. To bring wholeness and integrity to all areas of our lives. We're told, "Let us draw near to God with a sincere heart and with the full assurance that faith brings" (Heb. 10:22).

When you come to terms with the fact that you can't make life work on your own and you move beyond trying to fake it by default, then you're right where you need to be—dependent on God and his Spirit. We don't always like being there or feel comfortable being so vulnerable, but it's also liberating. We can let go of trying to make things happen and instead get on God's schedule and let him make things happen.

When I was an associate pastor in Baton Rouge, we were increasing the number of small groups we had, and I convinced a guy named Brian that he would be a good leader. It took my best stuff to convince him. On the night his group was to start, he ran back into his bedroom in panic and called me to tell me how afraid he was. He thought he could never do it, and he almost sold me on the idea. His wife finally dragged him back to the living room, where his first words were, "I quit. I can't do this. I resign and am going to give it to the Holy Spirit."

Something happened, and people were impressed by his transparency to the point of sharing personal things themselves. Two hours later, many of the attendees told Brian that they had never been to a better small group meeting and they couldn't wait to return. The group remained intact for many years, and on occasion Brian would open the meeting with a solemn face and tell everyone, "I resign."

Our sincerity and authenticity are not only qualities that God requires and honors. He also uses them in all our relationships. Our openness not only creates an open dialogue with our Father but also enhances our relationships with other people. Even if they don't like what we say, others will respect us if we are truthful, kind, and fearless. People love to feel confident and to be around someone who inspires them to be more confident and courageous.

When some people are discouraged, they bail out, looking for the closest exit to escape. However, others stay in there and fake it, pretending they have it all together when we all know it's impossible, like I did right after Bible school. Please don't be the type of person who does either. Please know that authenticity will take you farther and keep you stronger in your walk with God and others.

God wants all of us to rest confidently in the knowledge of his love and the hope we have in Christ. As a result of this kind of confidence, not only do we have the freedom to be ourselves, but we also have the privilege of sharing this freedom with others. We're free to fail, to shop for feminine products for our wife, to start over in business, to fall and get back up again. We're free to love because we have been loved by the source of all love.

We can be real because our confidence rests in him.

CONCLUSION

Real Hope for Real Change

As I shared at the beginning of this book, I was privileged to attend the finale of *American Idol* and see my friend Kris Allen win the whole shootin' match. I really do believe that Kris is a great example of someone who is true to himself and obedient to God's call on his life. He hasn't let success change his values or beliefs. He's remained focused on what it means to be real in a world that so often encourages us to be fake.

At the time Kris was competing, some people gave me flak for allowing one of our church's worship leaders even to audition for a show like that, let alone supporting him and celebrating his win. They would ask me, "Why would you throw a fellow Christian into the lions' den of pop culture? Why expose him to all the temptations that Hollywood and the music industry have to offer? Why endorse their worldly values at all?" For them, it was a matter of segregating a Christian from the vices of the world and protecting other Christians in the church from the worldly appeal of Kris's success.

My response to them was simple: "Because Jesus called us to share his message of hope throughout all the world, with all people—even those in Hollywood! And because apparently God called Kris to share his faith through this most unique opportunity." You see, I've never been someone who believes that God wants us to live in a bubble and protect ourselves from the culture around us. I believe he wants us to be salt and light in a world that's lost its flavor and is in the dark. I'm convinced he wants us to be a beacon of hope in a world that usually only sees the darkness of desperation.

He wants us to be real and rely on his strength, knowing that he will empower us to face any temptations that come our way. He wants other people to see his character reflected through us—in our words and our actions, in our attitudes and our habits, in our music and our artistry, in how we handle fame and success as well as adversity and hard times. When the source of our true identity is Christ, then we live with real hope and discover the freedom to be authentic. When we're real about who we are, the hope we offer is also real. And more than ever, everyone needs to be reminded of the power of hope.

AGAINST ALL HOPE

As we've seen, being real requires relying on God so that you don't have to rely on yourself or, worse, try to fake it. You're not limited by circumstances or forced to be a victim of painful events. You have a hope that is in the Lord. Scripture tells us, "The LORD is good to those whose hope is in him, to the one who seeks him" (Lam. 3:25). Paul writes, "May God, the source of hope, fill you with joy and peace through your faith in him. Then you will overflow with hope" (Rom. 15:13 GW).

> **Being real requires relying on God so that you don't have to rely on yourself.**

If we want to learn how to maintain hope through all the ups and downs of life, there's no better example than Abraham. As he pursued

God's plan, he had to wait and wait while watching everything go wrong that could go wrong. He made all kinds of dumb mistakes, but the one thing he never did was lose hope. Abraham was a hope junkie! "Against all hope, Abraham in hope believed and so became the father of many nations" (Rom. 4:18). This verse sounds like a contradiction, but it's not! It simply reminds us that even when it seems irrational, we must keep our hope in God.

Through old Abe's example, there are several other lessons we can learn about hope. First, we must take charge of our future and keep moving toward it. God told Abraham to leave the place where his father, Terah, had settled and head "to the land I will show you" (Gen. 12:1). Abraham wasn't even sure where exactly the Lord was leading him, but he knew he had to follow.

The same is true for us. God shows us each next step and asks that we trust him. It's like going camping when your kids are young. Inevitably, one of them has to go to the bathroom in the middle of the night, and there you are, leading them by the hand with only a flashlight to guide your next steps. They may be scared because they can't see where they're going, but they trust you and let you lead them where they need to go.

God blesses us when we take action and move in the direction he asks us to go.

I'm convinced that God blesses us when we take action and move in the direction he asks us to go. Every time God has blessed me, it's been on the move. Whenever I have a big decision to make, I think about it, pray about it, and talk to some other people about it. But it's only when I actually take steps toward his voice that God blesses me.

Abraham's father, Terah, had stopped short of where God had called him. He arrived in a village called Haran, which just happened to be the name of his other son who had died. Whether he was immobilized by grief over losing his son or just exhausted from the journey, Terah settled for less than where God wanted to lead him. When Abraham heard God leading him out of Haran, he had a big choice to make. He could follow his father's example and stay put. Or he could step out in faith toward the hope of his Father's calling.

We have the same choice before us each day. We can choose to settle and just get by, just keep our heads above water and survive another day. Or we can choose to take charge of our future by following God on the path of our divine destiny. We can play it safe, or we can take a risk and go for it.

Abraham took the risk and fulfilled the potential that God had created him for. "By faith Abraham, when called to go to a place he would later receive as his inheritance, obeyed and went, even though he did not know where he was going" (Heb. 11:8). God calls you to move boldly into your future and live out your inheritance. He asks you to act in faith to establish your legacy—something you may not see right away or even in your lifetime, but something that will last for eternity.

BETTER THAN GOLD

If we want to stay real and quit faking it, hope is our lifeline. But living with hope is not living without problems. Just because we have hope doesn't mean we won't struggle. In fact, no sooner had Abraham decided to take control of his future and follow God than he ran into problems. Right out of the gate, he discovered that there was a famine in the land, so he headed down to Egypt. I'm guessing that's not what he expected!

When you choose to follow God and try to be real, you can expect some bumps in the road. Sometimes it's just part of the journey, and sometimes it's our enemy escalating his assault on us. You know what I'm talking about, don't you? You go to the marriage retreat, dedicate your marriage to God like never before, and then come home and fight more than ever. You commit to honor God with your finances, and then something breaks down and you feel like you have no choice but to go in debt to get it fixed.

Why does it have to be this way? The answer is amazingly simple and yet not what we want to hear: pain is the high cost of real growth. If there's no pain, there's no gain. There are no five easy steps to a perfect life. Most of us want the finished product without the process. But the finished product requires maturity, stability, and wholeness. We can't short-circuit the growth process. We can't expect everything to be easy. Struggles and challenges are there not to wear us out but to strengthen us. The Bible says it this way: "This means tremendous joy to you, I know, even though you are temporarily harassed by all kinds of trials and temptations. This is no accident—it happens to prove your faith, which is infinitely more valuable than gold" (1 Pet. 1:6–7 Phillips).

Now, even a hope junkie gets tired sometimes. Vince Lombardi said it this way: "Fatigue makes cowards of us all." Abraham certainly experienced it. You know, you're trucking along and doing your best to follow God and obey his commands. You've come so far, yet it feels like you still have a long way to go. You get discouraged and don't know how to keep going.

These are the times when we have to lean on the Lord like it's nobody's business. (To be honest, God wants us to lean on him like that all the time, but we don't al-

> **Pain is the high cost of real growth.**

ways realize that.) You have to focus on where you're going and not where you've been. You have to stop saying that what you're facing is impossible and instead remind yourself of what Jesus said: "Everything is possible for one who believes" (Mark 9:23).

God has so many amazing promises about this for us in the Word that it doesn't hurt to remind you of a couple more! Luke 1:37 says, "For with God nothing will be impossible" (NKJV). Nothing! And look at this one—Matthew 7:7 says, "Ask and it will be given to you; seek and you will find; knock and the door will be opened to you." The more you *look* for God's promises when you're tempted not to overcome what seems impossible, the more you find! Mmm, God's Word is so good. You ought to read it sometimes. It's really, really good!

Okay, if that last challenge about everything being possible was too much of a stretch for you, at least try this. If you're at a place where you are stuck, saying, "I can't whatever" (you fill in what your whatever is), add the word *yet* at the end: "I can't _____ yet." Then add, "But with God . . ." But with God—that always changes things. Radically.

Our attitudes are important in shaping how we feel and the actions we take. We can choose to change our attitudes. I can remember being a kid and faking a stomachache so that I could take a sick day from school. Funny thing, though, was that sometimes by the end of the day, I really did feel sick. It's like the words on the tombstone of the hypochondriac: "See, I told you I was sick!"

HOPE MADE REAL

If you want greater hope in your life, then choose to believe and expect that God wants to help you and will. We're told, "Abraham never wavered in believing God's promise. . . . He was fully convinced that God is able to do whatever he promises" (Rom. 4:20–21 NLT). Even when he couldn't see what was around the bend, Abraham kept his faith alive.

Perhaps the most dramatic way that he kept his faith alive was by daring to believe that God would keep his promise and make Abraham the "father of many nations" (Gen. 17:4). The only problem, however, was that he and his wife, Sarah, were getting old and hadn't been able to have a baby yet. Common sense told him that it wasn't possible. Other people probably told him that it wasn't going to happen. Sarah probably said, "Don't even think about it!"

But he never gave up. "Without weakening in his faith, he faced the fact that his body was as good as dead—since he was about a hundred years old—and that Sarah's womb was also dead" (Rom. 4:19). Notice something very important here: Abraham didn't deny reality, he just denied the verdict. He didn't pretend to be happy with some kind of fake enthusiasm. He just quietly maintained faith in God to do what God said God would do.

It would be foolish for us to ignore the fact that sometimes we face enormous problems. However, we can be well informed without accepting a prognosis that we're doomed to defeat. Defying the verdict means that you refuse to accept that your marriage can never be fulfilling or that your business won't rebound. Defying the verdict means that you can acknowledge your fears and doubts without allowing them to consume your faith.

I believe we must actively engage in two things that will strengthen our faith, create enduring hope, and ultimately defy the verdict. The first is simply to keep our communication with God open and honest, which requires frequent prayer and frequent time in his Word. The second is that we must walk out what we see in the Word and hear in our conversations with God.

There are times when I want to pray and can't wait to pray. But there are other times when I don't want to pray. But one thing I know: I must never go through life thinking that I can go without spending time in prayer and in the Word. If it's good enough for Jesus, who *is* the Word, it's good enough for me.

There are two words for the word *word* in the Word! One is *logos* and the other is *rhema*. *Logos* means written word—powerful but incomplete. *Rhema* means the revealed Word that is tattooed on your heart and then becomes alive and real and powerful. This is where it starts counting—when it starts changing you. So, yes, having the Bible on your coffee table might be cool, but there's nothing to it until it gets inside of you, and then it's living and active and gives you power to move through life with confidence.

We must build our lives completely on the Word of God. It will inspire you, it will bring grace and truth to you, and it will change you. A lot of times people underestimate the power of the Word. But when Jesus was in a time of prayer and fasting, Satan showed up and started challenging Jesus with pride, trying to get him to sin. Each time Jesus spoke, he responded, "It is written." Satan tried to get him to eat something, and he responded, "It is written: 'Man shall not live on bread alone, but on every word that comes from the mouth of God'" (Matt. 4:4). He was speaking the Word, and the only way you can speak it is if you know it! You can't look at the enemy and say, "It is written: something about this ain't right!" You have to know it. You have to say something that is actually written in the Word!

When the Israelites were wandering around in the desert, they got enough manna for that day. In the spiritual realm, it works the same way: we get enough manna for the day. Tomorrow, our hands are empty! You start over every day. It's like being married. On Monday, I can show Michelle how much I love her all day long. But on Tuesday? It's bone dry. I have to start over every day!

This is the way it is with the Word of God. You receive it, but tomorrow you have to have more. He even taught us how to pray: "Give us today our daily bread" (Matt. 6:11). Our daily bread is for today. So I think God would want us to know this Word—his Word! His Word is all about him confiding in you his thoughts. They're clearly, plainly written down. You just have to read it.

I'd be lying if I said that reading the Bible is always easy and that I always get something out of it. Nope. Sometimes when I read it, three minutes later I'm so sleepy that I can't even remember what I just read. It helps to ask the Lord before you read to reveal what he has for you that day.

The more we are in the Word, the more we know what the Word says. The more we know what the Word says, the more in tune with the Father we will be when he whispers in our ear. He wants to tell you his secrets. You don't have to be a famous prophet like Elijah to hear what he has to say.

Isaiah 30:21 says this: "Whether you turn to the right or to the left, your ears will hear a voice behind you, saying, 'This is the way; walk in it'." God speaks to us today, just as he spoke to Elijah and Isaiah (see also 1 Kings 19:12). When you know what it is he is calling you to do, do it! Walk it out in your family relationships and in your workplace. Do what he is telling you to do.

God always keeps his promises. He kept his word to Abraham, and he keeps his word to you and me. "By faith Abraham, even though he was past age—and Sarah herself was barren—was enabled to become a father because he considered him faithful who had made the promise" (Heb. 11:11 NIV 1984). Abraham didn't rely on his own power because he knew he didn't have any in this case. He knew he was old and that his wife was not able to have children. But he also knew a greater truth. He "considered him faithful who had made the promise"! He knew that God would keep his commitment and do what he said he would do, somehow and some way, despite how stacked against it the odds were.

The same is true for us today. We have an amazing, all-loving, all-powerful God who wants to breathe new life into us and fill us with hope. He's calling you to your destiny and reminding you that you don't have to do anything you're not capable of doing. You don't have to be someone or something you're not. He has already placed within you everything you need to be real. This is how we succeed and flourish—by simply being who God made us to be.

So as we conclude our journey into what it means to be real, I remind you that God makes it simple for us. Being fake is exhausting, and it drains us and eventually kills our body and our soul. But being real requires us to put God first in our lives and to allow his love to overflow into every area of our lives. Our hope in him is real.

The more we put him first, give him our best, and love him completely and continually, the more we will enjoy his freedom like never before. We'll experience the abundant life, joy, peace, and contentment that God intended all along. We'll know our purpose and can follow God's call on our lives, serving him and advancing his kingdom.

The choice is yours and starts right now and every morning when you wake up. Do you want to live—to really live? Then you must be real. It's that simple.

Rick Bezet is the founder and lead pastor of New Life Church in Arkansas. With a God-breathed vision to reach Arkansas, Rick began planting churches throughout the state. Since he started NLC Conway in 2001, New Life has grown to include eight churches in seven cities with eighteen services and an online service. Rick speaks all over the world, inspiring and training church planters and leaders, but his heart is always to see the next person encounter Jesus. This passion led to the development of the Arkansas Dream Center, which serves thousands of individuals and families daily in local communities. Rick is a founding board member and overseer of the Association of Related Churches (ARC), an organization dedicated to planting life-giving churches across the nation.

Authentic relationships are the core of Rick's ministry. His desire to see genuine community grow helped develop the "life group" model that many churches use today. Even as more churches are planted, New Life remains one house, fully devoted to the ever-expanding vision of drawing souls to the hope of Jesus.

Rick and his lovely wife, Michelle, have four children and have been married for over twenty-five years. They live in Conway, Arkansas.

BE REAL

BECAUSE FAKE IS EXHAUSTING

SHARE YOUR OWN *BE REAL* MOMENT AT

WWW.RICKBEZET.COM

FREE BONUS CHAPTER, RESOURCES, AND MEDIA
AVAILABLE FOR DOWNLOAD

KEEP UP WITH RICK ON TWITTER @RICK_BEZET